D1617460

*Advances in Teaching Sign
Language Interpreters*

CYNTHIA B. ROY, *Editor*

Advances in Teaching Sign Language Interpreters

GALLAUDET UNIVERSITY PRESS
Washington, D.C.

Interpreter Education
A Series Edited by Cynthia B. Roy

Gallaudet University Press
Washington, D.C. 20002
http://gupress.gallaudet.edu

The illustrations on pp. 85 and 87 are from Mercer Mayer, *Frog, Where Are You?* New York: Puffin, 1969. © 1969 by Mercer Mayer. Reproduced by permission.

Library of Congress Cataloging-in-Publication Data

Advances in teaching sign language interpreters / Cynthia B. Roy, editor.
    p. cm.
  Includes bibliographical references and index.
  ISBN 1-56368-320-2 (alk. paper)
    1. Interpreters for the deaf—Education—United States. 2. Interpreters for the deaf—Training of—United States. 3. Sign language—Study and teaching—United States. 4. American Sign Language—Study and teaching. I. Roy, Cynthia B., 1950–

HV2402.A38 2005
419'.70802—dc22   2005040686

⊖ The paper used in this publication meets the minimum requirements of American National Standard for Information Sciences—Permanence of Paper for Printed Library Materials, ANSI Z39.48-1984.

CONTENTS

Contributors   vii

Curriculum Revision in the Twenty-First Century:
Northeastern's Experience   1
    DENNIS COKELY

Teaching Observation Techniques to Interpreters   22
    JEFFREY E. DAVIS

Discourse Mapping: The GPS of Translation   49
    ELIZABETH A. WINSTON AND
    CHRISTINE MONIKOWSKI

Beyond He Said, She Said: The Challenge of Referring
Expressions for Interpreting Students   78
    LAURIE SWABEY

Interpreted Discourse: Learning and Recognizing
What Interpreters Do in Interaction   100
    MELANIE METZGER

Teaching Interpreting Students to Identify
Omission Potential   123
    JEMINA NAPIER

From Theory to Practice: Making the Interpreting
Process Come Alive in the Classroom   138
    ROBERT G. LEE

Teaching Turn-Taking and Turn-Yielding in
Meetings with Deaf and Hearing Participants   151
    MIEKE VAN HERREWEGHE

False Friends and Their Influence on Sign
Language Interpreting   170
    ANNA-LENA NILSSON

Cold Calling? Retraining Interpreters in the
Art of Telephone Interpreting   187
    KYRA POLLITT AND CLAIRE HADDON
    WITH THE INTERPRETING TEAM OF THE
    UNIVERSITY OF CENTRAL LANCASHIRE,
    ENGLAND, U.K.

Index   211

CONTRIBUTORS

Dennis Cokely
   Northeastern University

Jeffrey E. Davis
   The University of Tennessee

Claire Haddon
   University of Central
   Lancashire, England

Robert G. Lee
   Boston University

Melanie Metzger
   Gallaudet University

Christine Monikowski
   National Technical Institute
   for the Deaf

Jemina Napier
   Macquarie University, Australia

Anna-Lena Nilsson
   Stockholm University,
   Institute of Linguistics,
   Department of Sign Language

Kyra Pollitt
   University of Central
   Lancashire, England

Cynthia B. Roy
   Gallaudet University

Laurie Swabey
   College of St. Catherine

Mieke Van Herreweghe
   Ghent University, Belgium

Elizabeth Winston
   Northeastern University

DENNIS COKELY

Curriculum Revision in the Twenty-First Century
Northeastern's Experience

IN THE SPRING OF 2001, Northeastern University's board of trustees approved a faculty resolution that the university convert from a quarter system to a semester system. Instead of four 11- or 12-week quarters per academic year, there would be two 15-week semesters and two intensive, 7½-week summer sessions. Most courses would be four credits, and students would normally carry sixteen credits per full semester. The board determined that the conversion would take place in the fall of 2003. This conversion afforded programs the opportunity to revise their curricula in whole or in part. The American Sign Language Program, already in the process of examining its language curriculum, decided to use this opportunity to revise its interpreting curriculum. The principals involved in the revision of the interpreting curriculum were Cathy Cogen, Robert Lee, and myself. We decided to base our revision on two primary factors, the theoretical and philosophical influences that had shaped our current curriculum and the extent to which our current curriculum prepared graduates for the types of interpreting situations into which they would be placed.

THEORETICAL AND PHILOSOPHICAL INFLUENCES

In 1983 the biennial Conference of Interpreter Trainers (CIT) in Monterey, California, invited educators from college and university

1

spoken-language-interpretation programs to share their experiences and perspectives on curriculum sequencing and assessment. This CIT, as well as presentations by spoken-language-interpreter educators at subsequent CIT and Registry of Interpreters for the Deaf (RID) conventions (see McIntire 1984, 1987), has had significant impact on the design and implementation of sign language interpreter training and education programs in the United States. It is ironic that in 1965 the first organization of sign language interpreting, the National Registry of Professional Interpreters and Translators for the Deaf, when searching for a new name, rejected suggestions from spoken-language interpreters that the name reflect the languages being worked with and instead changed the organizational name to RID. Among the significant new foci for sign-language-interpreter curricula after 1983 was the recognition of the usefulness and importance of translation and consecutive interpretation in enabling students to isolate and hone certain skill sets before they encountered the time pressures imposed by simultaneous interpretation. This recognition has led to a quite commonly accepted sequence of skill-set development (translation → consecutive interpretation → simultaneous interpretation) that in many programs takes the form of separate courses. The organizing principle underpinning this skill-set sequence is the gradual introduction of the pressures of real-time interpreting. In translation courses the production of the translation is fully separated in time (time shifted) from the production of the original. In interactions in which consecutive interpretation is used, the production of the interpretation is partially time shifted, and in simultaneous interpretation the production of the interpretation is in real time. Of course, because simultaneous interpretation is never temporally synchronous, there is a sense in which simultaneous interpretation is time shifted, at least at a micro, or phrasal or sentential, level. At a macro level, however, simultaneous interpreters create the illusion of temporal synchrony by striving not to alter the initial and terminal boundaries of interactions.

The focus on temporal synchrony was, in fact, at the core of the sequence of courses followed in Northeastern's interpreting curriculum before the year 2003. Specifically, our primary skill-development courses were American Sign Language (ASL) 1505, Translation; ASL 1506, Consecutive Interpretation; and ASL 1507 and 1508, Simultaneous Interpretation. However, twenty years and a new millennium after the 1983 CIT conference, emboldened by the opportunity to revise our interpreting curriculum, we determined that it was time to question whether the general organizing principles and sequencing of skill sets that resulted from the 1983 conference and that were widely accepted in sign-language-interpreting training and education programs remained meaningful for our curriculum and for the field.

Another characteristic of the curricula that grew out of the 1983 conference, perhaps influenced subtly by the experience of spoken-language interpreters, was a focus on monologue interpreting. Given that the ultimate goal of those spoken-language programs represented at CIT and RID conferences was—and remains—to produce graduates able to interpret simultaneously at international conferences, the focus of their curricula would logically be monologues. The extensive (indeed, almost exclusive) use of monologues in interpreter training programs in the decade preceding the 1983 CIT was also conditioned in large measure by several pragmatic realities of the time. First, the national certification test of the RID consisted exclusively of monologues (narratives and expository lectures). Not only was the RID evaluation composed strictly of monologues, but states focused almost exclusively on monologues as they began to develop their own screening processes. Because the goal of training programs was to produce graduates who would be judged qualified by RID or state screening bodies, programs responded accordingly. Curricula were shaped less by the actual communicative needs of d/Deaf people and more by the composition of the assessment instruments. In effect, this curricular focus on monologues was tantamount to "teaching to the test" rather than teaching to the task. Granting this much influence and control to testing procedures not rooted in basic research is highly problematic and has negative consequences for the Deaf community, as I have discussed elsewhere (Cokely forthcoming).

The second factor that contributed to establishing monologues as the norm in programs was economic. Before 1985 there were no commercially available materials developed specifically for sign language interpreting. (Sign Media's *Interpreter Models Series* would be the first videotapes commercially available for developing interpreting competencies.) Although the RID did release some of its older testing materials, they were not designed for instructional purposes and also were monologues. (One indication of how far the field has come is that the sign language source material in the original RID testing materials often consisted of memorized, signed versions of humorous written anecdotes from *Reader's Digest*, some of which entailed plays on words or puns.) Production of video materials in this period was still quite expensive, and multicamera materials were prohibitively so. The economic barriers to creating anything other than monologues were certainly a primary reason the RID evaluation materials were exclusively monologues; not only was using a single video camera to record material far less expensive than using multiple cameras, but editing monologue video footage was much less costly. In fact, not until 1988 did the RID test include an interactive dialogue situation as one-third of its performance testing conditions. In fact, to this day there are comparatively few commercially available nonmonologue materials (e.g., one-to-one interactions, group discussions) designed for interpreter training and education programs.

The relative ease with which a program could acquire or produce audiotapes and videotapes of lectures and other monologues and the type of materials used in RID evaluations also contributed to the emphasis on monologues. In addition, state and federal access legislation appropriately resulted in a marked increase in the number of conferences with d/Deaf presenters and attendees as well as the number of d/Deaf students attending postsecondary educational programs. Because formal interaction in such venues is perceived as decidedly monologic in nature, the focus on monologues as the dominant materials used in interpreter education and training programs became even stronger.

Ironically, although the field of interpreter training and education readily accepted a somewhat developmental approach to skill-set development (translation → consecutive interpretation → simultaneous interpretation), we sought no such developmental approach to the discourse settings in which interpreters would work. Among the unfortunate by-products of the focus on monologues in interpreter training and education programs was the misperception that the cognitive processes of interpreting when the source language is English are different from the cognitive processes of interpreting when the source language is ASL. This misperception has been perpetuated, perhaps subliminally, by certain courses (e.g., courses such as Sign-to-Voice Interpretation and Voice-to-Sign Interpretation) created in some interpretation programs.

The emphasis on monologues would seem to ignore the lessons to be learned from examining different paths one might take to become an interpreter. Elsewhere I have commented on the difference between a relationship to the community as a result of legacy and one as a result of reward (Cokely 2000). It is worth considering the legacy-or-reward distinction within the context of curriculum revision. Before the early 1970s, interpreters evolved from within the community; in other words, they had Deaf relatives or acquired their ASL skills from socializing with members of the community. These individuals were invited to or urged to interpret by members of the community. Importantly, their entrée into interpreting was almost exclusively in dialogue situations, usually beginning with telephone interpreting situations. Only after demonstrating their competence in such situations were they asked to or, in some cases, prodded to interpret in monologue situations. However, with the institutionalization of interpreter training and education and the focus on monologue interpreting, this natural evolution (and the wisdom of the community that it embodied) seems to have been forgotten or ignored. Inherent in this natural evolution is also the fact that "evolved interpreters" were thrust into situations in which interpretation could be viewed only as a unitary set of cognitive processes, and no artificial separation of cognitive processes into sign-to-voice and voice-to-sign interpretation was possible.

Just as modern Western medicine has begun to discover and accept the wisdom of the medicine practiced by peoples more closely tied to nature, perhaps those of us who are responsible for curricula in interpreter programs can rediscover the wisdom of the Deaf community when it comes to the development of interpreter competence. In fact, one could make an extremely convincing case that this community-based "introduction ritual" to interpreting, in which dialogues precede monologues, is born out by the underlying essence of communication. That is, communication is, by its very nature, an interactive, dialogic activity. Furthermore, dialogic interactivity provides a natural, interlocking, and interrelated series of exchanges that are extremely appropriate for developing competence in interpreting precisely, because those exchanges are somewhat self-defining. Quite simply, there is an expected routine and predictability to the way dialogic texts are executed (e.g., question-answer, statement-reply). Perhaps it is this very predictability that, in the collective mind of the Deaf community, made dialogic situations the acceptable entry point for "evolved" interpreters.

Although some hold that the presence of two interactants may seem to complicate an interaction from a sociolinguistic perspective, I suggest that what can be called "the power of two" actually serves to simplify and structure things from the student's perspective and from the perspective of educating and training interpreters. Consider that within a specific dialogic interaction (e.g., a phone call to make airline reservations), every question posed has only a limited set of acceptable and successful answers; every statement that is offered within that dialogic interaction has a relatively predictable set of appropriate and complementary responses. That is, for both d/Deaf and non-d/Deaf interactants, there is an inherent level of "success recognition" and "instant gratification" at multiple points of dialogic activity that cannot be easily or equivalently achieved within monologic activity. In addition, because there are numerous internal monitoring points within dialogues, the accuracy and success of an interpretation can be monitored by d/Deaf and non-d/Deaf interactants and their interpreter. It is precisely this ability to monitor success within and during an interaction that can and should be capitalized upon when working with students of interpretation.

After examining the theoretical and philosophical influences on our present curriculum, we concluded that the initial coursework in our revised curriculum should focus on dialogic interactions. That is, we would create a sequence of courses that would have the development of discourse competence as an organizing principle. We also determined that there was value in the commonly accepted skill-set sequence (translation → consecutive interpretation → simultaneous interpretation). We concurred with the prevailing thinking that this sequence of skill sets enables students to understand and manage the various cognitive demands placed on them as the time available within which to produce their work becomes constrained.

However, we also felt that separate courses focusing on these skill sets were no longer appropriate. Among our reasons was our clear sense that students perceived simultaneous interpretation as the ultimate goal of interpretation and that translation and consecutive interpretation were seen as means to that end. This perception was underscored by the very sequence of courses and prerequisites (the Consecutive Interpretation course had Translation as its prerequisite, and the first Simultaneous Interpretation course had Consecutive as its prerequisite). Thus we felt that students did not properly view translation and consecutive interpretation as strategies to be used in various interpreting situations but as mere stepping-stones to simultaneous interpretation. We concluded that each of the courses in our revised curriculum would include the accepted skill-set sequence (i.e., translation → consecutive interpretation → simultaneous interpretation). This plan, we believed, would greatly assist students in viewing translation, consecutive interpretation, and simultaneous interpretation as strategic tools to apply consistently or alternately within or throughout an interpreted interaction. However, we also realized that, in addition to having a solid theoretical basis, our curriculum revision had to be pragmatically grounded.

EMPLOYMENT SETTINGS

In addition to examining the theoretical and philosophical underpinnings of our new curriculum, we sought to determine the extent
to which it prepared our graduates for the real world of interpreting
they would face after graduation. For our students this meant becoming screened in the state of Massachusetts or attaining RID certification. All of our students take the written portion of the RID
examination before graduation. Given their level of success (to date
more than 90 percent of Northeastern students pass on the first attempt), we felt quite confident that in this regard the knowledge
base acquired by and displayed by our students was quite sufficient
and thus our content courses warranted little modification.

We were also concerned about our students' readiness to secure
immediate credentials needed to work in the state of Massachusetts
and surrounding states. In Massachusetts, screening is essentially a
two-step process—the first is an interview that assesses an appli-
cant's knowledge and ethical awareness; the second step, which can
be taken only several months after a candidate satisfactorily com-
pletes the interview portion, is a performance assessment. The
Massachusetts Commission for the Deaf and Hard of Hearing sets
aside special dates each spring for our seniors who will remain in
the state after graduation to take the interview portion before their
graduation. Again, 90 percent of our seniors to date have passed this
portion of the state screening on their first attempt, making us fairly
confident that the knowledge and ethical base acquired and demonstrated by our students was quite sufficient and that our content
courses needed minimal modification.

However, we wished to know whether the proficiency base provided to our students through our present interpreting curriculum
adequately prepared them for the interpreting opportunities that
would be available to them on graduation. To address this question,
we submitted a research proposal to the Commission, which, among
its many functions, serves as the only interpreter referral agency
in Massachusetts. Working with one of our graduates who had
recently been hired as a referral specialist by the Commission, we

proposed to categorize and analyze each referral made by the Commission within a six-month period.* We were particularly interested in those assignments that involved interpreters qualified by the Commission two years previously or less. We concluded that assignments given to interpreters within approximately two to three years after graduation would represent the types of work for which our students should be prepared. We concluded that our students, on graduation, should be able to handle successfully the types of assignments routinely given to interpreters qualified for two years or less.

During the six-month period studied, the Commission filled 1,474 requests for interpreting services. It should be noted that, given the severe shortage of interpreters and transliterators, a large number of requests went unfilled. In addition, the 1,474 requests that were filled did not include any public school requests since public school districts in Massachusetts do not contact the Commission to fill their classroom interpreting and transliterating needs. In addition, because colleges and universities with large d/Deaf-student populations, such as Northeastern University, Boston University, and Northern Essex Community College, employ their own full-time staff interpreters, they generally contact the Commission only when their own resources are insufficient.

The 1,474 filled requests for services were placed into one of three categories: one-to-one interactions, small-group interactions, and large-group interactions. One-to-one interactions were defined as those with one d/Deaf and one non-d/Deaf principal interactant (e.g., new-employee orientation, prenatal checkup, counseling session, learner's permit training). Small-group interactions were defined as those with between three and fifteen interactants (e.g., parent group discussion, individual education plan team meeting, staff meeting, advisory council meeting). Large-group interactions were defined as those with typically a single presenter and an audience of more than fifteen (e.g. professional conference, awards

---

* In order to maintain confidentiality, we ensured that the data collected contained no identifying participant or interpreter information.

Dennis Cokely

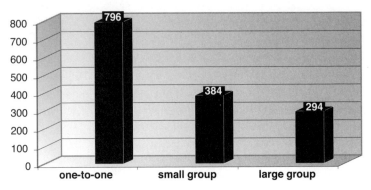

Figure 1. Distribution of all interpreting assignments

banquet, college graduation, memorial service). Figure 1 provides
the distribution of the 1,474 requests across these categories.

As figure 1 makes clear, 796, or 54 percent of the total requests
filled by the Commission during this period, were one-to-one interactions; 384, or 26 percent of the total requests, were small-group
interactions; and 294, or 20 percent, were large-group interactions.
Of the 1,474 assignments filled during this period, 368 assignments,
or 25 percent of the total, were filled by interpreters qualified for two
years or less. The assignment allocation distribution for interpreters
qualified for two years or less mirrors that for all interpreters, as
seen in figure 2.

As figure 2 indicates, 61.4 percent of assignments filled by interpreters qualified for two years or less were one-to-one interactions,
21.7 percent were small-group assignments, and 16.8 percent were
large-group assignments. It is certainly significant for curriculum
development purposes that one-to-one interactions accounted for
more than half of assignments for all interpreters and for more than
60 percent of assignments filled by interpreters qualified for two
years or less. In fact, one could argue that an inverse relationship
has evolved between the reality of assignment distribution and the
monologic focus seen in program curricula. In addition to categorizing requests by the level of discourse interactivity, requests
within each interactivity category were categorized on the basis of

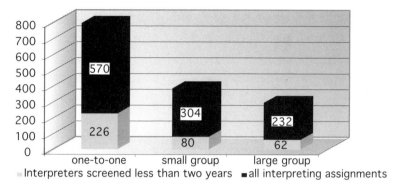

Figure 2. Allocation of assignments by experience

the general type of setting. These data were most helpful in providing a sense of assignment breadth and focus within the three interactivity categories.

The results of this analysis revealed that those individuals who had been qualified for two years or less were most often assigned to situations that can best be described as interactions that seek information (e.g., job interviews, job performance reviews, insurance case histories, medical case histories, prenatal checkups). The second-most-common placement was situations that could best be described as interactions that chronicle events (e.g., library story hours, twelve-step programs, insurance accident reports, testimonials). The third-most-common placement was situations that could best be described as expository presentations (e.g., college or university classroom lectures, museum tours and presentations, new program orientation training, diversity training). The fourth-most-common placement was situations that could best be described as interactions that seek to influence (e.g., sales pitches, political interactions, cochlear implant presentations, campaign kickoff events). These four categories accounted for more than 80 percent of all assignments (some of which were team placements with a Certified Deaf Interpreter colleague), not only for all interpreters, but also for those qualified for two years or less. Clearly some interpreted interactions represent complex combinations of these types. For

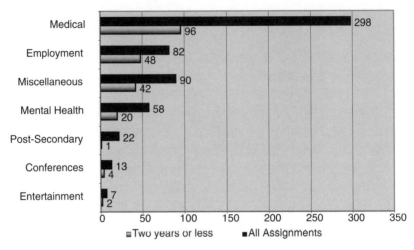

Figure 3. Settings for one-to-one assignments

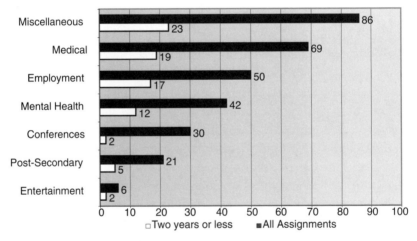

Figure 4. Settings for small-group assignments

example, a prenatal checkup might be categorized as an informa-
tion-seeking interaction. However, responses to questions within
the checkup might be presented as a chronicle of events, and the attending physician might then explain how to do a self-test and
might conclude the interaction by trying to convince the mother-
to-be of the importance and necessity of regular exercise.

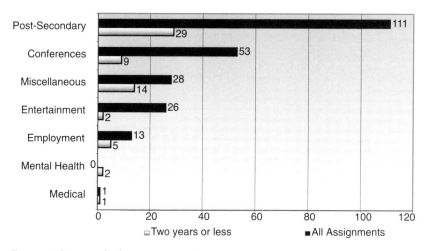

Figure 5. Settings for large-group assignments

   This analysis of assignment allocation and of settings by interactivity category revealed that our current sequence of courses, with its focus on the temporal distance from the source text, did not fully meet the theoretical or practical employment needs of our graduates. That is, our focus on monologues and the management of temporal pressure was not the best preparation for our students. Although we feel we had been doing quite a credible job of providing the opportunity for our students to acquire and develop the foundational competencies they would need for the long term, we felt we could be even more effective in assisting our graduates to function more successfully in those situations in which they were most likely to find themselves after graduation.

CURRICULUM REVISION

After analyzing the theoretical and philosophical influences on our curriculum and those discourse situations in which our graduates are likely to find themselves, we concluded that we had to redesign our interpreting curriculum. We determined that our four interpretation skill courses should focus on those types of interactions in which our graduates would be most likely to find themselves after graduation. We also concluded that separate courses in translation, then consecutive interpretation, and finally simultaneous interpretation did not adequately represent or prepare students for the workplace. That is, we determined that our students should come to think of translation and consecutive and simultaneous interpretation all as strategies to be used, when necessary and appropriate, within interpreted interactions. We therefore agreed that each of our skill-oriented courses would focus on translation, consecutive interpretation, and simultaneous interpretation and that the relative weight given to each skill set would vary by course. In other words, most of the first course might be spent on translation, with some attention to consecutive interpretation and simultaneous interpretation; most of the final course, however, might be spent on simultaneous interpretation, with diminishing emphasis on consecutive interpretation and translation.

In the most important departure from the past, we determined that our newly designed skill-set courses should focus on those interaction types the workplace data revealed to be most common: inquiry interactions, narrative interactions, expository interactions, and persuasive interactions. We determined that, unlike our previous curriculum, we would also require students to take a skill course, in addition to their practicum seminar, while they were on practicum. This arrangement would provide them with an ideal practice-oriented educational experience: interpretation difficulties and challenges encountered in the practicum workplace can be worked on in the classroom, and successes in the interpretation classroom can be transferred to the practicum workplace.

The four semester-long skill-development courses in our new curriculum are Interpreting Inquiry Interactions, Interpreting Narrative Interactions, Interpreting Expository Interactions, and Interpreting Persuasive Interactions. The relative and approximate percentage of course time spent on the temporal skill-set sequence within each course is shown in figure 6.

Figure 6 makes clear that each discourse-centered skill-development course will develop the students' ability to determine when

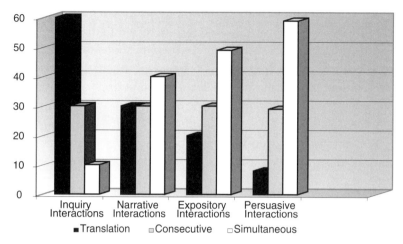

Figure 6. Percent of skill-set focus within courses

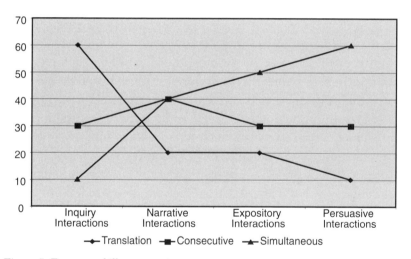

Figure 7. Focus on skill set over time

and whether to apply translation (including sight translation), consecutive interpretation, or simultaneous interpretation strategies to an interaction. The trajectory of focus on translation and consecutive and simultaneous interpretation over the four courses in our curriculum is shown in figure 7.

Figure 7 makes clear that students in each of the skill-development courses will focus on all the skill sets, but the relative weight given to each will vary from course to course. For example, in the Interpreting Inquiry Interactions course, approximately 60 percent of the content will focus on translation competence (e.g., translation of taped interviews, application forms, hospital admission forms), 30 percent will focus on consecutive interpretation competence (e.g., telephone interpreting, taped and live interview interpreting), and 10 percent will focus on simultaneous interpretation (telephone interpreting and taped and live interview interpreting).

We believe there are several levels of significance in this curriculum design. First, because translation, consecutive interpretation, and simultaneous interpretation are not segregated, students readily come to view each of them as viable strategies that can, and should, be adopted when and if appropriate. When presented with assignments in the classroom, they are able to practice and articulate the decision-making processes they employ in determining which strategy to use and are able to justify and explain their choices. Most importantly, they come to view simultaneous interpretation as only one of the work options available to them (albeit perhaps the most frequently employed option); they come to view translation and consecutive interpretation as viable, independent options, not mere stepping-stones to simultaneous interpretation.

Second, using the organizing principal of discourse rather than temporal control (a marked departure from accepted historic practice) creates an environment in which students focus on the typical and predictable characteristics of the most commonly occurring discourse types in which interpreters work. Students also come to realize that the complexity of certain types of interaction consists of embedded discourse types. For example, a speaker who is trying to persuade listeners to do something (e.g., vote for a particular candidate) may seek information about the listeners' economic status by asking a series of questions (inquiry); then the speaker may tell listeners about the predicaments of people faced with a different economic status (narrative); next the speaker may explain why the candidate will institute policies that will effect positive changes for all (exposition); the speaker may conclude by describing exactly what steps the listeners should take to recruit additional supporters for the candidate (procedure). With a discourse focus, students begin to understand the function of particular discourse types within the overall goal(s) of a given interaction.

Third, a discourse-focused curriculum has positive implications for assessing students' overall skill development. For example, during classroom activities in the Inquiry Interaction course, students analyze and practice program-produced videotapes of interpreted telephone interactions. However, students are given only the first two-thirds of each inquiry interaction; assessments then consist of the students' interpreting an entire interaction. Students are thus placed in situations in which they begin with maximum opportunity for success; the critical assessment point occurs when students are confronted with the "novel one-third." It is precisely this juncture that becomes critical in engaging students in analysis and discussion of their skill development. They enter this novel segment of the interaction maximally prepared to succeed: they know the overall purpose of the interaction; they are familiar with the interactants; they have specific background information with which to frame the remainder of the interaction; they have developed ways of communicating specific information; and they are in a position to maximize their predictive skills. This level of preparedness allows student and instructor to focus on the critical issues that arise when students truly must interpret.

Fourth, a discourse-focused curriculum has positive implications for the types of audio and video materials we both collect and develop ourselves for our extensive resource library. Because of this new focus, we have begun to view and allocate materials differently. In the past the temptation was to use the same materials twice, once in the consecutive course and again in the simultaneous course. The assumption (not unique to our program), not based on any empirical data, was that since the curriculum focus should be on control of time, the actual text or discourse material was secondary, and in fact, repetition of the same material was beneficial to the students. Using audio and video material twice (once in consecutive and once in simultaneous courses) was acceptable because temporal relation to source input was the primary curriculum focus. With a curriculum focus on discourse, however, material selection and use within courses is approached quite differently. Now we are more easily able to categorize the materials in our resource library. We have developed a database that categorizes our materials according to discourse type and can now choose video materials on the basis of the specific discourse characteristics they exhibit.

In addition to the changes in the skill-development courses, we made other adjustments to our curriculum. We reduced "Introduction to the Interpreting Profession" to a two-credit course, which enabled us to add another two-credit course, "Ethical Fieldwork." This course is designed to pair students with certified interpreters in various settings (freelance, agency, and educational) in what can be described as an ethical practicum course. The intent of this course is not for students to interpret but rather to shadow their senior colleagues for a semester and engage in analytic discussions regarding the range of practical, ethical pressures and decisions that must be made in the course of their work. This practical, real-world experience serves to inform the Ethical Decision Making course.

We have also introduced a Research Capstone course. Although students receive credit for this course in the fall semester of their senior year, the course actually spans 3½ semesters. In the fall of their junior year, students are paired with a faculty member to identify and select a research topic or question that is of interest to the student. During the next year or so the student will gather and analyze data and prepare a research report. Our intent is to hold an annual research symposium during the spring, to which interpreters in the area (including those interpreters who work with our students in their Ethical Fieldwork and Practicum courses) will be invited. Students will present their research findings, and our current plan is that students will interpret for their classmates as they present their research.

We have also taken the somewhat unusual step of introducing a skill-set course (Interpreting Persuasive Interactions) that is de-

Table 1. Revised Interpreting Course Curriculum

Year	Fall semester	Spring semester
Junior	The Interpreting Profession (2)	Interpreting Narrative Interactions (4)
	Interpreting Inquiry Interactions (4)	Advanced ASL 2 (2)
	Advanced ASL 1 (2)	
Senior	Interpreting Expository Interactions (4)	Interpreting Persuasive Interactions (4)
	Ethical Decision-Making (4)	Practicum (4)
	Ethical Fieldwork (2)	
	Research Capstone Course (4)	

signed to be taken while students are on practicum. Although we appreciate the scheduling difficulties this course may impose on students trying to fulfill their practicum requirements, we believe the new course will enhance our students' development. Not only will it provide a structured setting for students to continue to develop their skills, but more important, it will provide an opportunity for students to focus on their own personal, practical successes and challenges as experienced in the workplace environment.

Finally, we have altered the requirements for our practicum course. In the past we required students to log a specified number of hours in order to meet their practicum requirements. With our new curriculum focus on discourse rather than time, we adjusted our practicum requirements. We now require students to log a specified number of jobs in order to complete their practicum requirements. This requirement is in keeping with how interpreters actually approach (and bill for) their work, and it reinforces the focus on discourse. Thus students must log a minimum number of jobs per week. We have defined a job as any interpreted interaction lasting thirty minutes or longer. Although some interpreting assignments last fewer than thirty minutes (e.g., interpreted phone calls), the majority of interpreting assignments in our analysis lasted thirty minutes or longer.

Although we made other adjustments in our interpreting knowledge courses, none was as significant as the paradigm shift in our interpreting skill courses. We believe that this shift has resulted in a more integrated developmental approach to our students' skill development and better prepares them for the world of work they will face as interpreters. Table 1 illustrates the courses in the revised interpreting portion of our curriculum. The numbers in parentheses indicate the number of credits awarded for each course.

Conclusion

We used the semester conversion opportunity to examine the theoretical underpinnings of our interpreting curriculum. This examination, coupled with data from a study of the assignments in which relatively inexperienced interpreters were placed, led us to shift the focus of our coursework. Rather than organize our curriculum around the time available to produce a piece or work, we have organized our courses around the type of interactions students are most likely to encounter in the workplace after graduation. A significant benefit of this curriculum revision is that we are able to provide students with an overall theoretical and analytical framework with which they can begin to assess interaction types during their practicum experiences and beyond. By applying the various skill sets (translation, consecutive interpretation, and simultaneous interpretation) within each of the skill-set courses, our students will come to see each of them as practical strategies that can be employed in various work settings rather than as stepping-stones to interpreting simultaneously.

We believe that this new curriculum not only offers a more theoretically satisfying organizational foundation for interpreter education but also prepares our students to better serve the needs of the communities they will work in.

REFERENCES

Cokely, D. 2000. Exploring ethics: A case for revising the code of ethics. *Journal of Interpretation*.

————. Forthcoming. Shifting positionality: A critical examination of the turning point in the relationship of interpreters and the Deaf community. In *Sign language interpreting and interpreter education: Directions for research and practice*, ed. M. Marschark, R. Peterson, and E. A. Winston. Oxford: Oxford University Press.

McIntire, M., ed. 1984. *New dialogues in interpreter education*. Proceedings of the Fourth National Conference of Interpreter Trainers. Silver Spring, Md.: RID Publications.

————. 1987. *New dimensions in interpreter education: Curriculum & instruction*. Proceedings of the Sixth National Conference of Interpreter Trainers. Silver Spring, Md.: RID Publications.

JEFFREY E. DAVIS

Teaching Observation Techniques to Interpreters

Education is not preparation for life; education is life itself.
John Dewey
All human science is but the increment of the power of the eye.
John Fiske

OBSERVATION IS ONE of the hallmarks of professional work, and developing this expertise is a priority for most professions (e.g., teaching, medicine, psychology, counseling, human services, law, interpreting). Depending on the profession and theoretical orientation, there are various approaches to teaching and applying observation skills. Clearly, the observation techniques used by classroom teachers will be different from those employed by medical professionals. On the other hand, professions that involve very different work settings may share the same principles for conducting observation. Consider the observation techniques (e.g., participant observation

Many of the observation techniques described in this chapter were developed between 2001 and 2004 during the collaborative project between the University of Rochester Medical Center (UR) and the University of Tennessee (UT) and supported by the Fund for the Improvement of Post-Secondary Education (grant #P116B010927) from the U.S. Department of Education. I am extremely grateful to my UT faculty colleagues Marie Griffin and Carol LaCava for their exceptional instructional teamwork and to our UR faculty collaborators, Robert Pollard and Robyn Dean, for generously sharing with us their cutting-edge approaches to interpreter education. Special thanks to Ellis Bacon for discussing with me some of the ideas presented here and for providing a place up in the Great Smoky Mountains for me to write. I take responsibility for the "interpretations" presented in this chapter; any "miscues" are my own.

and ethnography) that have been developed and implemented by cultural anthropologists and that are applicable to other professions (e.g., medicine, journalism, sociology, interpreting). However, interpreters are not trained as anthropologists, and these techniques must be *specifically adapted to fit the world of interpreting work*. In one such approach, which will be highlighted here, Dean and Pollard (2001 and 2005) have developed a descriptive and analytic schema specific to interpreter work, and in collaboration with other interpreter educators and practitioners, they have adapted this framework to the education, observation, and supervision of interpreters (see Dean et al. 2004; Dean, Pollard, English 2004).

As an interpreter, teacher, and researcher for the past three decades, I have followed a multidisciplinary approach to enhancing my work, particularly in conducting observations, analyzing context, enhancing mentorship, and providing meaningful feedback. Fortunately, there is now a body of knowledge in the field of interpretation that clarifies the parameters of the interpreter's role, illuminates the realities of interpreting work, and suggests best teaching practices. Current research and innovative teaching approaches suggest there are better ways to address what we basically know. That is, the interpreted message is determined or at least largely influenced by contextual factors such as setting, purpose, and participants (see Cokely 1992; Metzger 1999; Napier 2002; Roy 2000b; Wadensjö 1994; Winston and Monikowski in this volume).

Along similar lines, Dean and Pollard (D and P hereafter) have presented a new approach to studying the interpreting context and have made a compelling case that in addition to language and culture, the work of interpreters is influenced by the demands of the physical environment, the interpersonal dynamics of the individuals present, and even intrapersonal factors. Although most would agree that awareness of contextual factors and discourse processes is critical to successful interpretation, the way we teach and acquire these skills is another matter. This chapter provides an overview of some observation and contextual analysis techniques relevant to interpretation and describes my experience using D and P's innovative approach to making observations and analyzing context.

OVERVIEW OF OBSERVATION APPROACHES

First, consider the ethnographic approaches first used by anthropologists to describe culture and now employed by several disciplines in the human sciences to describe the interrelationship between language and culture. How are these observational approaches best adapted for use by sign language interpreters? Traditionally, anthropologists and sociolinguists have followed an ethnographically based methodology to describe the interrelationships between languages and cultures (e.g., Geertz 1973, 1983; Hymes 1974; Saville-Troike 2003; Spradley 1979, 1980). Ethnography has been shown to be a powerful observation and descriptive tool, and this approach has been adapted to the study of interpreting contexts and used to gather information about the interpretation process (e.g., Simon 1994). For instance, discourse analysis employs an interdisciplinary approach and ethnography to study language use in specific communicative contexts. Three ethnographically based approaches that seem particularly relevant to observation and the study of interpreting contexts are discourse analysis (Schiffrin 1994), ethnography of communication (Saville-Troike 2003), and participant observation (Spradley 1980).

Discourse Analysis

Discourse analysis has been successfully applied to the study of interpreting contexts and specifically to teaching interpreters (e.g., Metzger 1999 and this volume; Roy 2000a, 2000b; Winston and Monikowski this volume). Discourse analysis can be broadly defined as "an examination of language-in-use or the study of actually occurring language ('texts') in specific communicative contexts" (Schwandt 2001, 57). Sociolinguists use ethnographic methodology and conversational analysis to observe the relationship between language and society and the ways various discourse features reflect certain social configurations. Metzger (this volume) proposes that "interpreters' work is discourse." Discourse analysis has contributed to our understanding of how the role of the interpreter is more than a passive and neutral conveyor of others' words and thoughts. Roy (2000a, 10) tells us, "Interpreting is a discourse process in which interpreters are active participants who need to know about and understand interactional behavior as well as explicit ways in which languages and cultures use language and how that changes our perception of what interpreters do." This perspective suggests that the ability to quickly survey and assess the multiple factors operating in a particular interpreting context is critical to successful interpretation and an expertise that is likely to be enhanced by developing keen observation skills. The notion of interpreter as active (or interactive) participant warrants further research and has implications for interpreter education. In sum, one interprets in context, not in a vacuum; thus context is a strong ally for an interpreter.

The Ethnography of Communication

The ethnography of communication (Saville-Troike 2003) explores how and why language is used and how its use varies from culture to culture. A central concept here is *communicative competence*, first introduced by Dell Hymes (1974), an anthropologist and one of the pioneers in the field of sociolinguistics. In essence, when we learn to use a language, we learn how to use it in order to do certain things that people do with language, and communicative competence accounts for this kind of ability. Gumperz (1972, 205) defines the term as follows: "Whereas linguistic competence covers the speaker's ability to produce grammatically correct sentences, communicative competence describes his ability to select, from the totality of grammatically correct expressions available to him, forms which appropriately reflect the social norms governing behavior in specific encounters." Subsequently, Hymes (1974) introduced an ethnographic framework, commonly known by the acronym SPEAKING, to describe contextual factors and the nature of the communicative message (see appendix). What Hymes makes clear is that there is more to understanding how language is used than describing the syntactic composition of sentences or specifying their propositional content. Getting students to focus beyond the word level is a major challenge for interpreter educators. Hymes's framework can be used to introduce interpreting students to the multiplicity of factors (e.g., setting, purpose, participants) beyond the lexical level that influence the outcomes of the interpreted message. Hymes's model is central to Saville-Troike's textbook (2003) *The Ethnography of Communication.* An example of how this ethnographic approach has been successfully adapted to the study of interpreting contexts can be found in the 2000 curriculum published by the National Multicultural Interpreting Project (NMIP), funded by the Department of Education. During the initial three years of the NMIP project, an extensive task analysis of interpreting in multicultural settings (where much interpreting work takes place) was undertaken. It was evident that interpreters working in multicultural settings must have keen observational skills. Recognizing this, the NMIP curriculum employed the ethnography of communication to increase interpreters' awareness of multiple contextual factors that exist across a range of multicultural settings (Mooney et al. 2000, 1–37).

Participant Observation

Participant observation is an ethnographic approach, recognized as the hallmark of cultural anthropology, that is now widely used as a method of research in numerous other disciplines (e.g., organizational communication, political science, sociolinguistics, education, sociology, medicine). The primary objective of this qualitative research approach is to gain valuable insights from the perspectives of the participants. Stated differently, it is a way to get inside the thought worlds of the participants. According to DeWalt and DeWalt (2002, vii), "participant observation has been used to develop this kind of insight in every cultural setting imaginable, from non-Western cultures little understood by Western social science to ethnic group and sub-cultural groups within North American and European settings." Participant observation is closely linked to ethnography and is an effective means of conducting fieldwork that involves developing keen observation skills, enhanced short-term memory, informal interviewing techniques, and special note-taking skills. The skills developed in this observation approach also have important relevance for interpreter research, education, and practice. For example, I have used Spradley's textbook (1980) *Participant Observation* to teach and study various contexts (including interpreting). Spradley combines ethnographic interviewing techniques with guidelines for participant observation to teach how to make ethnographic descriptions. This qualitative research methodology can be adapted to observe and analyze a variety of interactive contexts and applied to teach students, practitioners, and researchers to do ethnography through participant observation. This research method offers intriguing possibilities given the importance of observation for interpreters and the complex role of interpreters as active participants in the interpreted event. Professionals working on the front lines of a discipline can offer insights unavailable through other research approaches. In the field of education, we talk about the value of "teacher as researcher," and the same can be said about "interpreter as researcher." This principle is reflected in the present volume, in which the authors are practicing interpreters and teachers.

Rather than being an exclusive tool of anthropologists, ethnography has applications across the human sciences. "It is the one systematic approach in the social sciences that reveals what people think and shows us the cultural meanings they use daily" (Spradley 1980, vii). Ethnography provides in-depth observation analyses of contextual factors, which we know influence the outcome of the interpreted message. It offers a way for students of interpretation to learn that a high level of awareness of contextual factors is critical to interpretation/translation. Ethnography, of course, was designed more as a research methodology than as a way to teach interpreters. At the same time, it helps us sort through questions about interpreters as participants in what is typically a highly interactive communicative context. This process leads us to the notion of interpreting as a reflective practice. That is, interpreters must be ever vigilant as they work in a variety of contexts and encounter a multiplicity of factors (and demands). To be successful requires a high level of

sociolinguistic competency, contextual analysis skills, and the will-
ingness and ability to give and receive feedback. Having considered
these major observation-based approaches, I would now like to
share my experience and describe some of the benefits of using the
demand-control (D-C) schema designed specifically for analysis of
interpreting work.

THE DEMAND-CONTROL (D-C) SCHEMA FOR INTERPRETING WORK[1]

I have been studying and applying the D-C schema for interpreting
work since 2001. For interpretation to be successful, interpreters
must have the ability to quickly survey, assess, and deal with the
multiple factors evident in a particular interpreting context. I have
found that the D-C schema meets this need, is complementary to
the sociolinguistic approaches described above, and presents a co-
gent way to conduct observations and analyze contextual factors.
This pragmatic method links theory with professional practice, creating an awareness of the range of "control options" available to interpreters in response to a variety of contextual factors. Along with
the development of observational skills, this approach combines
teaching the value and consequences of various translation choices
with ethical and effective decision making. (See Dean and Pollard
2001, 2005; Dean, Pollard, and English 2004 for a more detailed account of D-C-based instructional approaches, especially observation-supervision.)

The EIPI Template

D and P designed the D-C schema to account in the broadest way
for the demands (contextual factors) encountered by interpreters.

---

1. The D-C schema for interpreting work was adapted by Dean and Pollard (2001, 2005)
from D-C theory based on occupational health research conducted by Karasek (1979) and
Karasek and Theorell (1990).

Stated differently, demands are contextual challenges (in addition to language and culture) that emerge in the course of doing interpretation. This idea forms the central tenet of the D-C schema. EIPI stands for the following categories of factors:

- Environmental (factors specific to the assignment setting, e.g., roles of the consumers, terminology specific to the setting, physical surroundings)
- Interpersonal (factors specific to the interaction of the participants, e.g., cultural differences, power dynamics, alignment issues, differences in funds of information[2])
- Paralinguistic (factors specific to the expressive skills of the d/Deaf and hearing consumers, e.g., style, pace, volume, accent, clarity of the linguistic forms that the interpreter hears and sees)
- Intrapersonal (factors specific to the physiological and psychological state of the interpreter, e.g., fatigue, physical reactions, distracting thoughts or feelings)

Controls of the Interpreter

Based on Karasek (1979) and Karasek and Theorell (1990), Dean and Pollard defined controls as follows: "Controls are skills, characteristics, abilities, decisions, or other resources that an interpreter may bring to bear in response to the demands presented by a given work assignment" (Dean and Pollard 2001). Control options employed by interpreters may include the following:

- education
- preparation for the assignment
- experience
- behavioral actions or interventions

---

2. *Funds of information* refers to the unique perceptions, preconceptions, and interactional roles of the consumers (cf. Pollard 1998). Along similar lines, D and P make frequent reference to *thought worlds*, a term taken from Namy (1977, 25), who wrote, "Interpreting is more than transposing one language into another. . . . It is throwing a semantic bridge between two people from differing cultures and thought worlds."

• positive self-talk
• translation decisions (examples presented later in chapter)

D and P define translation decisions as "specific word or sign choices or explanatory comments to consumers" what some might call linguistic and cultural adjustments. Positive self-talk is an instance of "the simple yet powerful act of consciously acknowledging the presence and significance of a given demand and the impact it is having on an interpreting assignment." D and P stress that "the term *control* is a noun, not a verb, and is preferably stated as *control options*" (Dean, Pollard, and English 2004, 67). In the D-C schema, the control options of the interpreter are divided into three major temporal categories:

1. Before the assignment (education, language fluency, and assignment preparation)
2. During the assignment (behavioral and translation decisions)
3. After the assignment (follow-up behaviors and continuing education)

Through EIPI analysis, students learn to describe and assess appropriate control options (i.e., evaluate their decision latitude) in response to the demands of an interpreting job. The EIPI template provides a framework for students, practitioners, educators, and mentors (and potentially consumers and professionals from other disciplines) to engage in meaningful dialogue about the outcomes of various actions and translation choices that emerge during interpretation. Designed specifically for the analysis of interpreting work, it has been shown to have application across a range of interpreting contexts. See Dean and Pollard (2005) for a more detailed description of the scope of the D-C schema and its numerous applications.[3]

---

3. Faculty training is critical to the successful application of the D-C schema. For information about training opportunities and research in the D-C schema for interpreting work, see http://www.urmc.rochester.edu/dwc/news.htm.

Curricular Collaboration and Implementation

From 2001 to 2004, faculty from University of Rochester Medical Center (UR) and the University of Tennessee (UT) were involved in a collaborative project titled Reforming Interpreter Education: A Practice Profession Approach.[4] The purpose of this three-year project, supported by the Fund for the Improvement of Post-Secondary Education, was to implement the D-C schema for interpreting work throughout UT's baccalaureate interpreter preparation program (IPP) curriculum and evaluate its effectiveness. As the project progressed, a number of other IPPs and interpreter mentors also began employing elements of the D-C schema (see Dean, Pollard, et al. 2003). Five courses were developed or adapted by UR researchers and implemented by UT faculty. The highlight of the UR-UT project has been the implementation of observation-based coursework designed to enhance students' interpersonal skills and ethical and translational decision-making skills, and to provide a realistic understanding of the contextual factors that impact interpreting work (see Dean and Pollard 2005; Dean, Pollard, and English 2004; Dean, Davis, et al. 2003).

Observation Enhancement

Most interpreter training programs introduce students to observation by encouraging them to participate in Deaf community events and to observe interpreters working in a variety of public settings. Sometimes these assignments involve interviewing the interpreter or Deaf people at the event and writing a report that may or may not include students' observations. These assignments tend to focus on observing the interpreter or understanding the signed message, and sign choices and signing styles receive much attention. Certainly, language immersion and cross-cultural experience are essential to

---

4. For a description of this project, see: http://www.urmc.rochester.edu/dwc/scholarship/Education.htm.

the development of linguistic and communicative competence. At the same time, we must give full consideration to the best ways to develop in-depth observation and contextual analysis skills across a variety of potential interpreting scenarios during pre-service training.

The observation, practicum, and supervision hours required by other professions (e.g., teaching, medicine, and law) far surpass those required in interpreter training. To help address this apparent gap in interpreter education, the D-C schema incorporates an observation-supervision teaching tool adapted from problem-based learning (PBL). This educational approach is in line with a growing movement away from teacher-driven (didactic) classrooms and toward student-driven education (see Dean and Pollard, 2005). The PBL movement in medical education "was developed in response to the critique that newly graduated physicians were lacking in their ability to interview and diagnose patients (interpersonal skills) and their ability to critically think through patient care and treatment decisions (judgment skills)" (Dean et al. 2004, 152). In a PBL approach, first-year medical students might, for example, learn medical information contextually (i.e., through interactive involvement in patient cases). Observation-supervision[5] is a central tenet in the D-C schema and reverses traditional educational approaches (supervision is commonly used in the practice professions and will be discussed later in this chapter). Rather than starting from the point of memorizing terminology and the code of ethics and moving toward context, interpreting students are first immersed in real-world settings and are encouraged to derive terminology and translation questions from these firsthand observations across a variety of contexts (even when no d/Deaf people are present). This approach enables students to analyze the demands (job requirements) and controls (decision making) relevant to future interpreting scenarios in which they may be involved, and it provides a common language

---

5. "Observation-supervision posits that, in light of the more holistic view of interpreting work emphasized by the D-C schema, learning about specialty content work (e.g., legal, medical, mental health) is optimized by being in those specific environments and understanding the goal of those environments, the characteristics and motivations of the people present, and the typical communication exchanges that occur in those settings" (Dean, Pollard, Davis et al. 2004, p. 152).

and fosters a safe and meaningful learning environment among students and between learner and teacher, mentor, and supervisor. The objective is for students to gain valuable insights into the "funds of information" brought to the situation by key participants. Observing, analyzing, and engaging in such meaningful dialogue about interpreting work is an alternative to the "sink or swim" approach that is commonly found in the field (see Dean and Pollard 2001 and 2005).

Demand-Control Coursework

The first D-C course in an IPP was team taught by UT faculty Marie Griffin and me with instructional support provided by Robyn Dean. In this course, students were first introduced to the D-C schema and were taught how to apply the schema to a variety of contexts. The students used a series of exercises called situational analyses, including stimulus material in the form of pictures, television show segments, videotaped material, guest lectures, or events in the community (moving gradually from noninterpreted to interpreted events). Judging from the students' performance and feedback, this application of the D-C schema enhanced observation skills through the EIPI analysis of hypothetical interpreting contexts. These activities increased the students' awareness of the control options available to interpreters in response to certain contextual demands, thus enhancing their critical decision-making skills. The noninterpreted events were expanded into "hypothetical interpreting assignments" in order to help student quickly identify contextual demands and discuss the available control options. Observation opportunities in the first D-C course were made available in a variety of ways:

- observation material provided by the teacher or the student
- observation material reviewed either for one specific demand category or for the entire D-C spectrum of EIPI demand categories and control options
- in-class (simulated), or out-of-class (in-vivo) activity
- large-group or small-group activity;

Keep in mind that although the D-C instructional activities described below were implemented in the IPP at UT, these activities have also been widely used in other instructional formats (Dean and Pollard, in press; Dean et al. 2004).

During the UR-UT project, it became evident that the D-C schema could be presented in what Dean et al. call "four distinct elements" (2004, 151).

1. A *theoretical construct* (i.e., its conceptual framework, rationale, principles, and terminology)
2. A *dialogic work analysis* (i.e., situational analyses expanded into hypothetical interpreting settings in which students consider both positive and negative consequences relative to control options, thus enhancing critical thinking and decision making)
3. A *learning tool* (i.e., PBL-style and observation-supervision)
4. An *assessment tool* (Dean and Pollard, 2005)

The D-C schema as a theoretical construct and dialogic work analysis can be introduced during any foundation course, such as principles of interpreting or introduction to interpreting. Dean, Pollard, Davis, and colleagues (2004, 153) report that "unlike the first two D-C schema elements, PBL-style courses and observation-supervision *require significantly more teacher training and adaptation or augmentation of the curriculum*" (my emphasis).

The situational analysis activities showcased in this chapter were designed by Robyn Dean for the first Application of D-C Theory to Sign Language Interpreting course offered at UT. The faculty has subsequently used these activities in other courses, such as the summer Basic Interpreter Training Program. After a description of these instructional activities, I will discuss my experience with the D-C schema as a learning tool.

SIMULATED OBSERVATION ACTIVITIES

Picture analysis is an in-class simulated observation tool that can be introduced early in the semester. It was first developed by D and P as a way to teach the analysis of the EIPI demand categories in various interpreted settings. This instructional technique has been successfully demonstrated in various workshops around the country, such as the 2001 Registry of Interpreters for the Deaf (RID) Conference, and in the first D-C course taught at UT. For the picture analysis, the instructor or the students bring in pictures, from magazines or other sources, that look like a potential interpreted setting. The instructor and the students create an interpreting scenario to go along with a picture. Various people in the picture are assigned specific roles (e.g., the interpreter, consumers who are Deaf and those who are hearing, other participants, etc.). After the students are presented with the picture stimulus and scenario, they are asked to predict and discuss the potential EIPI demands that might emerge. Students can work in groups to analyze the picture and accompanying scenario for different EIPI demands. There are several variations of this exercise. For instance, each group can focus on a different EIPI demand category for a more in-depth analysis. Students are asked to consider this question: "How would the EIPI demands affect your job?" After a comprehensive EIPI analysis is accomplished, the controls before, during, and after the assignment are discussed. The picture analysis activity has the following objectives:

- teach the application of EIPI analysis to interpreting scenarios
- develop observation skills
- enhance prediction skills in preparation for interpreting work
- increase understanding of the demands encountered during interpreting work
- introduce students to control options that are available to interpreters

Another simulated activity for situational analysis is the *television show excerpt*. Students use a segment from a television program or movie to practice demand-control analysis. For example, in the first D-C course, Robyn Dean provided the instructors with excerpts from the television show *ER*. In this case, most students were familiar with the characters and story line. To facilitate this type of situational analysis, the instructor provides the hypothetical scenario and

chooses the excerpt for the class to watch. (Students could also analyze a television show excerpt as a homework assignment.) To get
the activity started, students describe what they know about the
backgrounds of the main characters (race, ethnicity, professional
training, significant others, etc.) and discuss what is currently happening in the character's life. This is an excellent activity to help
students understand what it means to get inside the thought world
of the participants.

Creating another scenario from the clip, the instructor (or students) can specify who the Deaf person might be in each scenario.
Introducing a hypothetical Deaf character and interpreter into the
scene dramatically shifts the perceptions of demands and opens up
the discussion for other considerations. This is an excellent activity
for highlighting environmental demands (specific to the emergency
room setting in this case) and interpersonal demands (interpreting
for the patient, family members, health-care worker). Video clips
that illustrate paralinguistic and intrapersonal demands can also be
selected to give the full range of potential demands that might be
encountered. This is a good "drill" activity to teach students to
quickly observe and assess the demands of a situation they walk into.

Expert groups are another way to apply the D-C schema and
EIPI analysis. Naturally, it may be overwhelming at first for an individual student to concentrate on all four demand categories simultaneously. A way around this problem is to divide the class into
"expert groups" and assign one of the EIPI demand categories to
each group. Concentrating on a single demand category allows
students a more in-depth analysis, and working in a small group
demonstrates what is possible given adequate time, attention, and
teamwork. A similar outcome is achieved by assigning individual
students to focus on one demand category. As students gain expertise with the analysis and become more confident, they will be able
to examine all four demand categories simultaneously and readily
apply this observation skill to a variety of settings.

The war story analysis is useful later in the semester, after students are comfortable with applying the D-C schema to a variety of
settings. This activity is a good way to get students to consider the

demands and controls of a specific interpreted setting involving Deaf consumer, hearing consumer, and interpreter participants. In this activity, the instructor invites a working interpreter to class as a guest speaker (and fully informs the interpreter of the purpose for the visit). The instructor requests that the guest interpreter come to class prepared to share a true story (or two) of a challenging interpreting assignment. As the guest interpreter shares a story, students (individually or in small groups) begin to list the specific demands (in written notes or on the blackboard behind the speaker) that are evident in the story. Dean (reported in Davis and Griffin, 2002) proposed this activity as a way to get students to think on their feet.

Although it may seem somewhat risky to share so-called war stories with beginning interpreting students, the UT instructors found this activity to be one of the most beneficial offered in the D-C course (Davis and Griffin 2002). The feedback we received from the guest and from the students in the class echoed this opinion. The guest was impressed by the depth of analysis demonstrated by the students, and the students reported that they appreciated knowing up front some of the challenges encountered during interpreting work and felt most of them could be addressed through the application of appropriate controls.

Other variations on this activity are to invite a variety of guests (e.g., a spoken language interpreter, a Deaf consumer of interpreting, a hearing consumer of interpreting, etc.) at different times to share their experiences with the class. Teachers might consider telling their own interpreting stories to allow the students to practice the D-C analysis before inviting guests. The RID *Views*, other RID publications, and Mindess (1999) are good sources for additional scenarios. Incidentally, our class guest told us that he was not distracted by the students' writing down the EIPI demands on the board behind him as he lectured. In this approach, space is given on the board for each EIPI demand category, and one student is assigned to concentrate on each category. The students must recognize and write down the demands in their category that emerge from the guest interpreter's story. Each student is given the opportunity to ask the guest interpreter questions about the demands and

discuss controls that were or were not applied. Ideally, the guests
will share what they might have done differently before, during, and
after the assignment. This may not be comfortable for all guests,
however, and the nature and purpose of the activity should be described at the time the invitation is extended. As a follow-up activity
during a subsequent class session, Marie Griffin and I (2002) suggest "red-heart interpreting" stories (stories that demonstrate how
interpreting is rewarding despite the challenges). Students expressed appreciation for having a variety of perspectives presented.

   During the first D-C course, students were also required to complete a series of out-of-class observations. Students observed several
events that were not interpreted or based in the Deaf community.
Each of the following types of events was observed: (a) an off-
campus event, (b) a cross-cultural event, and (c) an interactive group
meeting. The purpose was for the students to learn to apply the
principles of the D-C schema to a variety of real-world monologic
and interactive contexts that might hypothetically be interpreted.
To summarize, both in-class and out-of-class observation activities
were used to introduce students to the D-C schema. First, the EIPI
analysis was practiced in class with various videotaped or simulated
materials and hypothetical interpreting scenarios. Second, the EIPI
analysis was applied to a range of noninterpreted events outside
class. As observations progressed, students began to consider the
range of control options that would be available had these events
actually been interpreted. Finally, students practiced applying the
D-C schema to an interpreted event in the field. For the final observation assignment in the first D-C course offered at UT, students
worked in groups to conduct a full-scale EIPI analysis for a community-based interpreted event (e.g., city, county, or state government
public forum, local deaf service center or state commission for the
deaf event, religious service, theatrical production, etc.). Throughout the project, a four-step learning approach was followed (learning, applying, integrating, and demonstrating).

   For the final assignment, the students presented the D-C schema
and analysis to different groups of working interpreters at the uni-

versity and in the community. That is, teams of students prepared and made a group presentation on what they learned from the D-C course. The audiences for the students' presentations were as follows:

- educational interpreters for kindergarten through high school
- postsecondary educational interpreters
- the local RID chapter professional meeting at the community outreach program for the Deaf
- a group of local interpreters specializing in interpreting in religious settings
- a class of beginning interpreting students enrolled in the Principles of Interpreting class

Marie Griffin and I were present at each of the student team presentations. D and P attended the presentation to the Principles of Interpreting class. Some of the professional interpreters attending the students' presentations reacted as follows (Davis and Griffin 2002):

- "Didn't expect to learn from students' presentations but actually learned a lot"
- "Impressed with the level of sophistication and depth of analysis of students' discussions of the work"
- "This all seems so obvious, so why didn't I think of it before?"

Teaching Interpreting Specialty Courses via Observation-Supervision

The next two courses offered during the UT-UR project were Medical Interpreting and Educational Interpreting. Both were taught by means of PBL and observation-supervision. UT students enrolled in these two courses had already mastered the D-C schema during the first course in the sequence. Thus they were prepared to use it to analyze a variety of real and potential interpreting contexts "unencumbered by interpreting responsibilities (as in a practicum/internship)" and not "blinded by a singular focus on sign vocabulary (as with observations of working interpreters)" (Dean, Davis, et al. 2003, 1).

For example, in the Medical Interpreting course, students shadowed physicians during appointments with hearing patients at the UT Medical Center. Course participants were "exposed to basic medical knowledge, varied medical settings, and typical doctor-patient interactions and conversations through direct observation, in contrast to the superficial, non-contextualized learning that takes place through traditional classroom or workshop instruction methods" (Dean, Davis, et al. 2003). Robyn Dean made the logistical arrangements with the Medical Center and designed the course, and after each series of observations, students would research relevant medical information that emerged during the medical appointments. Students were encouraged to "use medical dictionaries, texts, and medical websites to further their understanding of anatomy (e.g., what does the liver do?), medical procedures (e.g., what happens in an angioplasty?) and more" (Dean, Davis, et al., 2003, 10).

Class time for the medical course was conducted as a "group supervision meeting."[6] *Supervision* here means "a regularly-scheduled time when advice and guidance is given, in order to address specific practice challenges and decisions or professional development in general. The interpreting profession uses the similar but less formal construct of mentorship." The instructor responds to "students' questions and promotes their understanding of the interpreting practice implications of their observation recordings" (Dean, Davis, et al. 2003, 10). For both the Medical Interpreting and the Educational Interpreting courses, Dean developed special observation forms, based on the D-C schema, for students to document, analyze, and report their observations. Then, during the group supervision sessions, students discussed these observations and were guided by the faculty to "consider a range of potential re-

---

6. *Supervision* (a common term in the practice professions) is used by D and P to describe one of *the most critical elements of applying the D-C schema as a learning tool* (see Dean and Pollard 2005; Dean et al. 2004).

sponses, including translational, attitudinal, and behavioral options. This fosters an open discussion about the implications or consequences of such decisions, in contrast to a rigid, unhelpful focus on *right and wrong*" (Dean, Davis, et al. 2003, 11). The medical course benefited the students by affording them the following opportunities (Dean, Davis, et al. 2003, 11–12):

In class, students and faculty discuss translation choices (and their implications) for doctor's statements and questions such as:

- At your next appointment, you must provide us with ejaculation fluid.
- I'm sorry. There is nothing more we can do for your mother but we will try to make her comfortable.
- This medication is better for you because it is short acting and safer.
- Are you feeling dizzy, is the room spinning, or are you light-headed?

And we discuss options for responding to scenarios like:

- Where do you stand during a treadmill stress test so you can be seen?
- What if the doctor continues to talk to a patient who is coming in and out of consciousness?
- What if the patient has raised a concern about being discharged from the hospital but the doctor doesn't seem to hear or acknowledge it?
- How can you show the concern and empathy that the doctor displays vocally and through intonation in a visual manner?
- How does translation time lag and time elongation affect the people and their interactions and how can the negative impact of that be lessened? (12)

In addition to the benefits of discussing these translation, attitudinal, and behavior responses, this training approach has numerous other benefits:

Students are interacting and working with patients and medical professionals. Witnessing medical appointments helps students to develop a comfort level and respect for the vulnerable position patients

are placed in when their personal medical history is discussed and
physical exams/procedures are performed. They also are privy to the
unique perspective of the physician (their communication goals,
their ethical dilemmas, their frustrations, etc.), which will help them
in their future interpreting work. Lastly, the students have the
unique experience of seeing themselves as "practice professionals"
working alongside other practice professionals (Dean, Davis, et al.
2003, 12).

My experience with the application of observation-supervision
through the D-C schema is that it provides instructors, supervisors,
mentors, and interpreting students new and meaningful ways to
make decisions and explain their work. Perhaps most important,
the students can see how their decisions, like those of physicians,
teachers, and other professionals, have consequences, and the exchange of ideas with their colleagues will help them assess those
consequences.

CONCLUSION

The central theme of this chapter has been the importance of observation for professional development of interpreters. Various observation techniques, including ethnographically based approaches
such as discourse analysis, participant observation, and ethnography
of communication offer valuable contributions, and a new approach
to interpreter preparation, the D-C schema for interpreting work, is
an excellent way to teach observation skills. Although these approaches represent somewhat different theoretical orientations,
they are complementary and significantly contribute to our understanding of the interpreting context. During a three-year collaborative project, the D-C schema was successfully implemented in the
IPP at UT. The UT interpreting faculty sees the pedagogic applications of the D-C schema as spiraling and ongoing. Numerous other
IPPs, interpreter educators, and mentors around the country have
started employing elements of the D-C schema in teaching, mentoring, and supervising interpreters. (See Dean, Pollard, and English

2004 and Dean et al. 2004 for much more information about these activities.)

Observation-supervision similar to that used in the practice professions (e.g., education and medicine) provides a way for more experienced professional interpreters to observe and assess the performance of entry-level interpreters, and vice versa (i.e., it offers a linkage between preservice and in-service training). This linkage enhances professional development, competence, and consumer protection (Dean and Pollard 2005). The D-C schema offers an important and often missing link between the classroom and the field. Developed specifically with interpreting work in mind, it provides a highly practical framework and common language that is applicable across a variety of interpreting settings (educational, medical, mental health, legal, vocational, etc.) and useful to both preservice and in-service interpreting levels. A major highlight of the D-C schema is that it reverses traditional approaches. Rather than starting from the point of rote memorization of specialized vocabulary and ethical tenets and moving toward context, the D-C schema is student driven and context centered. That is, students are immersed in real-world settings and encouraged to derive terminology and translation questions from observations across a variety of contexts. In addition to the numerous benefits described in this chapter, the D-C approach also:

- Informs teaching, practice, and research
- Complements other approaches (e.g., discourse analysis and service learning)
- Enhances other skills known to be critical to effective interpreting (e.g., note taking, translation, exegesis, critical decision making, etc.)
- Applies to a variety of specialized settings (educational, medical, legal, etc.)
- Fosters teamwork, mentoring, and practicum experiences
- Encourages consumer education and professional collaboration
- Contributes to train-the-trainer efforts

In conclusion, no one method offers a panacea. However, techniques that are solidly grounded in theory and research are needed to enhance the way we teach and work as interpreters. Although interpreter preparation should help lay a solid foundation for professional development, the realities of interpreting work contexts (and the participants therein) also determine to a large extent how much one grows as a professional interpreter. This is the unique contribution of observation—to understand interpreting in specific contexts; to predict challenges, conflicts, and concerns that might arise in the field; and to design a professional development plan (for self-improvement) based on that understanding. This is why observation is so critical. It cogently reveals the patterns of best practice that professional interpreters use to meet the challenges raised by working in a diversity of contexts in order to successfully interpret.

REFERENCES

Cokely, D. 1992. *Interpreting: A sociolinguistic model.* Burtonsville, Md.: Linstok Press.

Davis, J., and M. Griffin. 2002. The University of Rochester-University of Tennessee collaborative project. Paper presented at the biennial conference of Postsecondary Education Programs. Kansas City, Mo.

Dean, R. K., and R. Q. Pollard. 2001. Application of demand-control theory to sign language interpreting: Implications for stress and interpreter training. *Journal of Deaf Studies and Deaf Education* 6 (1):1–14.

Dean, R. K., J. Davis, H. Barnett, L. E. Graham, L. Hammond, and K. Hinchey. 2003. Training medically qualified interpreters: New approaches, new applications, promising results. *RID Views* 20 (1):10–12.

Dean, R., R. Q. Pollard, J. Davis, M. Griffin, C. LaCava, and K. Hinchey. 2003. Reforming interpreter education: A practice-profession approach —Years 1 and 2 progress report. Presentation at the biennial meeting of the Registry of Interpreters for the Deaf, Chicago, Ill.

Dean, R. K., R. Q. Pollard, J. Davis, M. Griffin, C. LaCava, B. Morrison, J. Parmir, A. Smith, S. Storme, and L. Suback. 2004. The demand-control schema: Effective curricular implementation. *Proceedings of the biennial meeting of the Conference of Interpreter Trainers*, 145–61. Silver Spring, Md.: CIT.

Dean, R. K., R. Q. Pollard, and M. A. English. 2004. Observation-supervision in mental health interpreter training. *Proceedings of the biennial meeting of the Conference of Interpreter Trainers*, 55–75. Silver Spring, Md.: CIT.

Dean, R. K., and R. Q. Pollard. 2005. Consumers and service effectiveness in interpreting work: A practice profession perspective. In *Educational interpreting: From research to practice*, ed. M. Marschark, R. Peterson, and E. Winston, 259–82. New York: Oxford University Press.

DeWalt, K. M., and B. R. DeWalt. 2002. *Participant observation: A guide for fieldworkers*. Walnut Creek, Calif.: AltaMira Press.

Geertz, C. 1973. *The interpretation of cultures*. New York: Basic Books.

———. 1983. *Local knowledge: Further essays in interpretive anthropology*. New York: Basic Books.

Gumperz, J. J. 1972. Sociolinguistics and communication in small groups. In *Sociolinguistics: Selected readings*, eds. J. Pride and J. Holmes. Harmondsworth, England: Penguin.

Hymes, D. 1974. *Foundations in sociolinguistics: An ethnographic approach*. Philadelphia: University of Pennsylvania Press.

Karasek, R. A. 1979. Job demands, job decision latitude, and mental strain: Implications for job redesign. *Administrative Science Quarterly* 24: 285–307.

Karasek, R., and T. Theorell. 1990. *Healthy work: Stress, productivity, and the restructuring of work life*. New York: Basic Books.

Metzger, M. 1999. *Sign language interpreting: Deconstructing the myth of neutrality*. Washington, D.C.: Gallaudet University Press.

Mindess, A. 1999. *Reading between the signs: Intercultural communication for sign language interpreters*. Yarmouth, Maine: Intercultural Press.

Mooney, M., A. Aramburo, J. Davis, T. Dunbar, A. Roth, and J. Nishimura. 2001. *National multicultural interpreting project curriculum*. Stillwater: Oklahoma State University.

Namy, C. 1977. Reflections on the training of simultaneous interpreters: A metalinguistic approach. In *Language interpreting and communication*, ed. D. Gerver and H. W. Sinaiko, 25–33. New York: Plenum.

Napier, J. 2002. *Sign Language interpreting: Linguistic coping strategies*. Coleford, U.K.: Douglas McLean.

Pollard, R. Q. 1998. Psychopathology. In *Psychological perspectives on deafness*, Vol. 2, ed. M. Marschark and D. Clark, 171-97. Mahwah, N.J.: Erlbaum.

Roy, C. B. 2000a. Training interpreters—Past, present and future. In *Innovative practices for teaching sign language interpreters*, ed. C. B. Roy, 1–14. Washington, D.C.: Gallaudet University Press.

———. 2000b. *Interpreting as discourse process*. New York: Oxford University Press.

Saville-Troike, M. 2003. *The ethnography of communication*. 3rd ed. Malden, Mass.: Blackwell.

Schiffrin, D. 1994. *Approaches to discourse*. Oxford, U.K.: Blackwell.

Schwandt, T. A. 2001. *Dictionary of qualitative inquiry*. 2nd ed. Thousand Oaks, Calif.: Sage.

Simon, J. 1994. An ethnographic study of sign language interpreter education. Ph.D. diss., University of Arizona.

Spradley, J. P. 1979. *The ethnographic interview*. New York: Holt, Rinehart, and Winston.

———. 1980. *Participant observation*. New York: Holt, Rinehart, and Winston.

Wardhaugh, R. 1998. *An introduction to sociolinguistics*. 3rd ed. Malden, Mass.: Blackwell.

Appendix

The Ethnography of Communication (Hymes 1974, quoted in Wardhaugh 1998), "The SPEAKING Acronym"

The Setting and Scene (S) of speech are important. Setting refers to the time and place, i.e., the concrete physical circumstances in which speech takes place. Scene refers to the abstract psychological setting, or the cultural definition of the occasion. The Queen's Christmas message has its own unique setting and scene, as has the President of the United States' annual State of the Union Address. A particular bit of speech may actually serve to define a scene, whereas another bit of speech may be deemed to be quite inappropriate in certain circumstances. Within a particular setting, of course, participants are free to change scenes, as they change the level of formality (e.g., go from serious to joyful), or as they change the kind of activity in which they are involved (e.g., begin to drink or to recite poetry).

The Participants (P) include various combinations of speaker-listener, addressor-addressee, or sender-receiver. They generally fill certain socially specified roles. A two-person conversation involves a speaker and hearer with no role change; a political speech involves an addressor and addressees (the audience); and a telephone message involves a sender and a receiver. A prayer obviously makes a deity a participant. In a classroom a teacher's question and a student's response involve not just those two as speaker and listener but also the rest of the class as audience, since they too are expected to benefit from the exchange.

Ends (E) refers to the conventionally recognized and expected outcomes of an exchange as well as to the personal goals that participants seek to accomplish on particular occasions. A trial in a courtroom has a recognizable social end in view, but the various participants, i.e., the judge, jury, prosecution, defense, accused, and witnesses, have different personal goals. Likewise, a marriage ceremony serves a certain social end, but each of the various participants may have his or her own unique goals in getting married or in seeing a particular couple married.

Act sequence (A) refers to the actual form and content of what is said: the precise words used, how they are used, and the relationship of what is said to the actual topic at hand. This is one aspect of speaking in which linguists have long shown an interest, particularly those who study discourse and conversation. Others too, e.g., psychologists and communication theorists concerned with content analysis, have shown a similar interest. Public lectures, casual conversations, and cocktail party chatter are all different forms of speaking; with each go different kinds of language and things talked about.

Key (K), the fifth term, refers to the tone, manner, or spirit in which a particular message is conveyed: light-hearted, serious, precise, pedantic, mocking, sarcastic, pompous, and so on. The key may also be marked non-verbally by certain kinds of behavior, gesture, posture, or even deportment. When there is a lack of fit between what a person is actually saying and the key that the person is using, listeners are likely to pay more attention to the key than to the actual content, e.g., to the burlesque of a ritual rather than to the ritual itself.

Instrumentalities (I) refers to the choice of channel, e.g., oral, written, or telegraphic, and to the actual forms of speech employed, such as the language, dialect, code, or register that is chosen. Formal, written, legal language is one instrumentality; spoken Newfoundland English is another; code-switching between English and Italian in Toronto is a third; and the use of Pig Latin is still another. In Surinam a high government official addresses a Bush Negro chief in Dutch and has his words translated into the local tribal language. The chief does the opposite. Each speaks this way although both could use a common instrumentality, Sranan. You may employ different instrumentalities in the course of a single verbal exchange of some length: first read something, then tell a dialect joke, then quote Shakespeare, then use an expression from another language, and so on. You also need not necessarily change topic to do any of these.

Norms of interaction and interpretation (N) refers to the specific behaviors and proprieties that attach to speaking and also to how these may be viewed by someone who does not share them, e.g., loudness, silence, gaze return, and so on. For example, there are certain norms of interaction with regard to church services and conversing with strangers. However, these norms vary between social groups, so the kind of behavior expected in congregations that practice "talking in tongues" or the group encouragement of a preacher in others would be deemed abnormal in a "high" Anglican setting. Likewise, an Arab and an Anglo-Saxon meeting for the first time are unlikely to find a conversational distance that each finds "comfortable."

Genre (G), the final term refers to clearly demarcated types of utterance; such things as poems, proverbs, riddles, sermons, prayers, lectures, and editorials. These are all "marked" too. While particular genres seem more appropriate on certain occasions than on others, e.g., sermons inserted into church services, they can be independent: we can ask someone to stop "sermonizing"; that is, we can recognize a genre of sermons when an instance of it, or something closely resembling an instance, occurs outside its usual setting.

ELIZABETH A. WINSTON AND
CHRISTINE MONIKOWSKI

Discourse Mapping: The GPS of Translation

> Whatever one may say about the inadequacies of translating, it is and continues to be one of the most important and honorable occupations in the world.
>
> *Goethe in a letter to Carlyle, 1827*

THIS CHAPTER describes an approach to teaching translation using discourse mapping. Elsewhere (Winston and Monikowski 2000) we presented a comprehensive description of discourse mapping and described a series of spiraling activities. It is a process that helps students and working interpreters render a successful message and includes "(1) accurate content; (2) appropriate context; (3) appropriate linguistic form" (16). Using discourse mapping activities, interpreting students learn to work from the known to the unknown, from analyzing the source to assessing the adequacy of the target. "By creating an actual map of a text, students can see the relationship of its three perspectives: content, context, and form" (17). Feedback from interpreter educators and working interpreters about the effectiveness and usefulness of discourse mapping has been overwhelmingly positive. Educators can guide students to develop skills that can be applied in class and, what is more important, that can be transferred to actual interpreting assignments. Working interpreters have reported using maps to assist their teammates while interpreting challenging texts; the process of creating a map clarifies the text and also helps explain why an interpreter may be struggling with a particular content, context, or form.

Translation is a foundational skill for interpreters. The process of translation provides interpreters with the opportunity to analyze, research, and assess both the source message and the target they produce. "The basis for using translation techniques in interpreter preparation is that translation provides an important framework for teaching and learning the interpreting process" (Davis 2000, 109). This process, without the pressure of time that comes with simultaneous or even consecutive interpretation, builds confidence in the interpreter's ability to understand and produce a clear message. Davis (114) also reminded us that translation activities in the classroom are "excellent way[s] to teach the importance of context and culture . . . and how to go beyond the lexical level to deeper levels of cultural and linguistic meaning." Discourse mapping is a particularly effective strategy for teaching translation. It leads interpreters through the translation process, from analysis of the source to production in the target language and finally to effective assessment of the translations they produce. We will discuss the application of discourse mapping to translation and demonstrate its effectiveness when used to teach translation.

REVIEW OF DISCOURSE MAPPING

Explanation of the Process

Discourse mapping is a complex, multistep approach to text analysis that an interpreter uses to change a message from source language to target language. It presents an in-depth, layered analysis of the underlying coherence of the text and includes an understanding of the content (themes, topics, and events), the context (register, settings, speaker's goals, etc.), and the linguistic form (discourse structures, transitions, vocabulary, etc.). "Mapping a text provides us with a clear picture of the underlying structure of that text and of the challenges it poses" (Winston and Monikowski 2000, 18). By creating numerous maps in a step-by-step, methodical way, interpreters (as well as instructors and students) can monitor the process of interpretation rather than assess only the end product. "The ultimate goal of discourse mapping is to give students a complete process that they can actually apply to the interpretation of any text" (57). The practice of discourse mapping can help students develop a variety of skills, including the following: prepare for comprehension (by brainstorming), enhance comprehension (intralingually and interlingually), build analytical skills (by assessing their production), and prepare and produce a target with adequate equivalence (18).

Other uses of mapping, both in general and in interpreting, were reviewed in our earlier work. Since that publication, we have received many anecdotal reports about the application of both the overall process and parts of it, and we know that many instructors have expanded pieces of the overall process as they adapt it to teaching their students. The overall process begins with a specific brainstorming activity, moves through intralingual maps that address comprehension and production of retellings in the same language, then spirals to interlingual maps that inform translations, consecutive interpretations, and simultaneous interpretations. As a final step, "discourse mapping becomes an effective tool for evaluating the adequacy of an interpretation" (Winston and Monikowski 2000, 22). At each step along the way, the instructor guides students through the process, ensuring comprehension, not only of the text, but also of the process (if the process is to become an internalized analytical tool, as is our goal). Once the student has developed successful mapping skills, different steps of the overall process can be selected for specific activities. For example, students may map each other's simultaneous interpretations to provide feedback in a group. This could lead to discussion of the overall success of several interpretations despite the differences rendered in the details. Or instructors' mapping skills can guide them to decide what texts are appropriate for a certain course or workshop. Mapping a text allows one to see the relative complexity of a text's structure and to

compare the underlying content structures, the context interrelationships, the linguistic features of the source, and the possible/probable (improbable) target language structures. Once we have this information, choosing texts for students becomes easier, and the chosen texts are more likely to meet the needs and abilities of our students. (Winston and Monikowski 2000, 56)

Goals of the Process

The goals of discourse mapping are to guide students to identify the overall structures within a text, to create meaningful visual representations of those structures, and to find structures in the target language that will adequately represent the message. It begins by presenting a clear understanding of the source text, which leads students to produce a successful target. "Discourse mapping leads them to an understanding of the larger context and discourse structures of the text; by understanding these, they can develop analytical skills for zeroing in on the meaning of single vocabulary items. In other words, it helps them understand the meaning rather than the words" (Winston and Monikowski 2000, 19). In addition, each step in the process has specific goals and objectives that complement the activity.

TRANSLATION

The Process

Larson (1984, 3) offered a definition of translation: "Translation . . . consists of studying the lexicon, grammatical structure, communication situation, and cultural context of the source language text, analyzing it in order to determine its meaning, and then reconstructing this same meaning using the lexicon and grammatical structure which are appropriate in the RECEPTOR LANGUAGE and its cultural context" (her emphasis). This is an essential foundational skill for sign language interpreters, and "the best practices in interpreter preparation" (Davis 2000, 111) must include translation as an explicit part of the educational process.

One challenge in translation is the one-to-many-and-many-to-one dilemma, wherein a single lexical item in the source language must be translated into one of several choices in the target. Davis provides several examples to support the "from one to many and from many to one" (118) characteristic of languages. The classic example between American Sign Language (ASL) and English is the English word *run* and the variety of possible ASL choices. This example clearly illustrates "that translation involves a great deal more than the simple replacement of lexical and grammatical items between languages. . . . Therefore, in order for meaning to be conveyed, the interpreter/translator must transcend the purely linguistic surface forms by way of *linguistic and cultural mediation*" (Davis's emphasis; 119).

The complex process of interpreting needs to be rooted in translation. It allows for time and analysis, the interpreter's two most precious tools. The process of analyzing the source text is a skill that needs to be honed by practice, support, and more practice. And the skill to render that source into an adequate target text requires the same amount of practice, application, and more practice. If one is to become truly successful when working simultaneously, then time and energy are required, and translation is the key to internalizing that process.

Equivalence/Adequacy

A discussion of equivalence is problematic because "it leads one to believe there is only one right way to interpret a text" (Winston and Monikowski 2000, 47). Rather, target texts approximate more or less the meaning intended by the originator. Equivalency is a relative term, being determined in part by the goals of the speaker and in part by the goals of the audience. For example, if the translator believes that the speaker and the audience want the translation to evoke similar feelings and recollections, the word/sign choice, discourse structure, and tone will be very different from those of a translation aimed at providing the audience with insight into the grammatical workings of a source language. And it will again be different if the goal is to provide access to technical information and terms that are essential in the source language but nonexistent in the target language.

Several researchers have taken a clear stand on the importance of meaning over form. Seleskovitch (1978, 98) states that "what the interpreter says is, in principle, independent of the source language." Wadensjö (1998), in providing an excellent historical review of definitions of equivalence, emphasizes the essential consideration of the situated discourse and its translation. Any translation must be assessed within its context and with consideration of its impact on the recipients as intended by the speaker. She writes, "When analyzing equivalency between utterances (i.e., comparing originals and translations) on the basis of the function(s) they are designed to perform, I am more or less consciously taking into consideration contextual aspects manifest in the situation" (43). Our approach to equivalence follows that of researchers who, like Wadensjö, look at the equivalence of target functions rather than target words. Her concern, like ours in using discourse mapping, is to have target texts that reflect the goals and intentions of the source.

Whatever the terminology, Larson's three classic questions (1984, 49) need to be addressed when one interprets a text: Is the meaning of the target language the same as that of the source language? Is the message clearly understood by the audience for whom the message was intended? Is the form natural? How to adequately answer these three questions, however, is the difficult part.

When discussing translations, Larson (1984, 489) offered five ways to test the quality of a translation: "1) comparison with the source text, 2) back-translation into the source language, 3) comprehension checks, 4) naturalness and readability testing and, finally, 5) consistency checks." She stated that "a careful comparison with the source text will need to be made several times during the translation process" and explains that this multiple-check approach addresses "information content" as well as linguistic form.

One objection to discourse mapping activities we hear from both students and instructors is that it is not possible "in real life" to actually map a source text because of the time constraints. Of course not! This is an activity meant to develop skills. Cardiac surgeons do not have time during operations to practice cutting blood vessels, sewing stitches, and reading instruments. Given this lack of time, should they skip the hours of practice needed to develop each skill and just try it all at once on a patient? And try it again, and again, until maybe somebody actually survives the procedure? Not our doctors, thank you! The tedious hours of practice on each discrete skill build the physician's abilities to manage the entire process successfully during real surgery. Working on specific steps of the interpretation process is no different. Students need time to practice and integrate each step repeatedly and successfully. Focusing heavily on the foundational step of translation is essential.

The failure to provide students with focused translation activities can be compared to growing tomatoes. Healthy tomato plants need good soil; the right amounts of sun and water; and protection from severe weather, insects, and diseases. If any one of these is missing, the plant may still produce tomatoes, but chances are the fruit will be too small or tasteless or will suffer from rot, bugs, or mold. When we eat such tomatoes, we might cut out bits and pieces and get the sense of a tomato, but the complete tomato is not experienced. We believe this analogy applies to students. If they do not give sufficient focus to analyzing the source and the target languages for meaning, if they leap into simultaneous interpreting of entire events straight out of ASL classes, if they do not have enough ASL (not to mention English) to analyze meaning, they will inevitably produce interpretations that are too sparse and too far from the source, provide little sense of the source, and are rotten in large areas. The consumers will not experience complete and successful communication.

What We Did and Why We Did It

Translation in the Discourse Mapping Process

The goal of activities focused on translation within the greater discourse mapping approach is to "produce accurate and complete target texts based on source text discourse maps" (Winston and Monikowski 2000, 34). Mapping activities for translation practice can include preparing and reviewing maps of the source text and maps of the students' retellings, analyzing sequencing and structures to present the message in the target language, analyzing effective linguistic features to present in the target language, and building students' confidence in their skills: memory, analysis, feedback, and production (35).

In this chapter, we will discuss a series of activities (and the assessment of those activities) that we chose to use in teaching experienced interpreters how to map for translation. Their goal was to eventually use discourse mapping as a tool when mentoring other interpreters working on meaning analysis. Meaning analysis is most effectively worked on with the time and resources available in translation.

Our Students

In an attempt to endorse the value of practicing translation within the discourse mapping approach, we elected to isolate that one step of the entire process and work with experienced interpreters. The activity was conducted with two separate classes. The students in each class were similar in background and experience. They were students in the third semester of a mentoring program and shared the goal of learning ways to provide mentoring in guided skill development approaches. The students in both classes, all of whom were experienced professional interpreters, had little or no experience with translations (either as students or as instructors).[1] The process was the same for each group. First, a videotape[2] was shown three to five days before it was discussed in class. The students were not told that it would be used for a specific translation activity. The objective of the preshowing was to give the students time and dis-

---

1. Students were enrolled in the Master Mentor Program through the University of Colorado/Boulder; they were in the third in a series of four courses. This course was a hybrid and had both a face-to-face and an online component. Two cohorts participated in the translation activity: one in June 2002 and one in June 2003. The students were all experienced interpreters and many were already involved in mentoring and/or instruction.

2. Mike Kemp, "See Now, Never See Again."

tance from the source text (which was signed) so that they would forget the specific signs but recall the concepts and ideas of the text itself. This, we hoped, would lessen their reliance on signs and increase their reliance on, and their confidence in, their memories and their ability to discuss the text using their own signs. We expected that the time and distance would result in eventual translations to English that used native English structures and vocabulary rather than attempts to match single signs to single words.

Random Concept Map

After the three to five days, we introduced the activity of mapping the text.[3] We conducted this as an intralingual activity, using ASL because it was the same language as the source text. We began by asking the students as a group to generate a random concept map. Our goals were to have students working together to generate memories of the text, to have them see a variety of signs and ways used to express the ideas of the original source, and to have them think more freely about the ideas without influence from the source language. When various students contributed their own recollections in ASL, the others were exposed to their peers' understandings of the story as well as a variety of ways to sign about them.

We chose to use drawings and pictures for the map rather than words or glosses (see figure 1). (Of course, glosses are also symbols, as are words; the drawings and pictures are simply less-language-driven symbols.) Drawings and pictures distanced the students even further from the source signs and resulted in a visual representation of the source. One point to emphasize at this stage is that the goal of a random concept map is simply to note as much of the text as the instructor chooses to include. A single picture may evoke an entire segment for some students. For example, in figure 1, the "restau-

---

3. In fact, if we could have had a longer period, weeks to months, we believe the resulting activity might have been even more effective in accomplishing the objective of distancing from the source.

2003

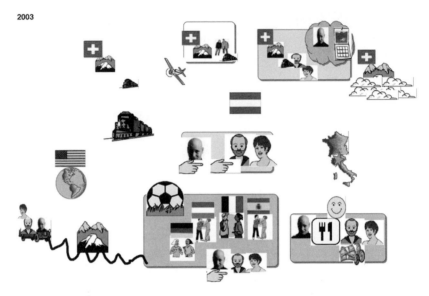

Figure 1. Random concept map

rant" symbol (knife and fork in lower right corner) was all that was needed to remind them of the entire dining event in the source text.

It is always the choice of the instructor whether to write glosses (English words) or use pictures on the random concept map. However, our goal for this specific activity was to stay as far from language-driven symbols as possible. And because this was a translation exercise, we could also have moved directly from the ASL source into English words on the random concept map, which may be more effective for more experienced interpreters. However, we have found using English words at this early stage often restricts the later translation. For example, writing "bumpy and curvy" on the random concept map may well have quashed the creative thinking that later resulted in "hair-raising." No one approach is correct. One approach may work better for one group than for another. The real lesson here for instructors and interpreters alike is to keep experimenting to see what works with particular groups. As always, it is important that instructors be clear about what they wish to accomplish by this activity. Conversely, if instructors are not sure what might be achieved through the activity, they need to be open to analyzing the outcomes and discussing with the students where and how the activity resulted in positive and negative outcomes.

While creating this map, the students included what they thought important, and the instructors made every effort to keep students focused on the major events of the story rather than bogged down in tangential details. The pictures were purposely placed randomly in the space in order to maintain the distance between the source sequencing and the map. The objective was simply to generate all the major concepts of the source, with some level of detail about each. This was sometimes a challenge because students see different things in any and every videotape; however, the group discussions were extremely helpful. Because the discussions were in ASL, students could repeat what they saw in the source text and seek clarification, they could use their own sign choices to explain their choices, and they could react to comments from their peers. These activities matched the objectives for this step in the discourse mapping structure; students needed to rely on their memories, their analytical skills, their production of ASL, and their feedback if they were to participate fully in this discussion of the source text.

Sequential Map

After everyone was relatively satisfied with the map and the level of detail, a sequential map was created from the seeming chaos of the random concept map. Again, the instructors guided students to a successful product, but more importantly, the instructors focused on the process of constructing a logical meaning. Tremendous detail is unnecessary in the sequential map. In one class we numbered the major concepts in chronological order; in the other class, we simply added arrows to show how we intended to sequence the events. In both classes, discussion ensued! We have included a rendition of the sequential map with arrows as figure 2.

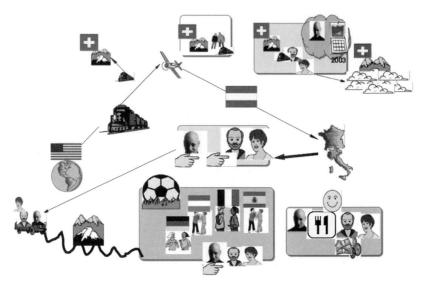

Figure 2. Sequential map

The Translation

Students then were required to prepare a translation from the sequential map alone. They were each given a copy of the class-created sequential map and instructed to write an English translation during a forty-five-minute period. This was an individual activity. When it was completed, the class came together for further discussion and comparison. We will discuss examples from these translations in the next section.

THE RESULTS

Assessing Translations with Mapping

One interesting and valuable application of discourse mapping throughout the teaching process is that it supports the assessment of student work. Teachers can compare student maps to their own, and students can compare their maps to the teacher's or to each other's. For discourse mapping to help teachers assess student work effectively, however, two essential things need to be determined: (1) the specific objectives of the teaching activity (what we intend the students to be able to do by the end of it and, therefore, what we will assess); and (2) the meaning of equivalency and adequacy.

Specific Objectives for an Activity

As interpreting educators, we have long accepted that there is no single "right," exactly equivalent, or perfectly adequate translation of a source text. Yet how often do we provide students with direction about the goal of our exercises and the type of equivalency or adequacy we are looking for at any given time? We must identify the goals and objectives we have established for our activities. Too often, we assign an activity because it is "like" interpreting or because we had to do it in our interpreting programs or because it "feels right." And also too often, we have no clear idea what we expect to happen at the end of these activities. If all seems to go well, we are pleased; if not, we have little idea of why, what to fix, and how to approach the activity or the skill development differently.

This does not mean that the activities have no merit; they may be excellent, if only we knew what for! They might be well fitted for advanced students but not appropriate for students beginning the learning process. Or they might be great for beginners, too, if only they were broken down into manageable steps. But until we have clearly defined the goals and objectives of each activity and informed the students what they are, we cannot claim to be teaching. We are only mixing up magic potions to see what effects they have on students.

Equivalence

In assessing student work, as discussed earlier, it is also always necessary to specify the level of equivalency we are expecting. Although our end goal may be to produce a translation and eventually an interpretation (with all the major topics, all levels of supporting detail, etc.), this may not be the goal of each individual activity as we progress through a series of skill development activities.

For example, beginning interpreters may need to focus on producing target texts that contain the major points but not many supporting details (similar to summaries or abstracts). As students gain skills and confidence, the level of detail we expect may increase. Most instructors we know have some system of evaluating target texts this way. But how do we define the goals and details? If instructors map the text and arrive at a linear map of the source text, they have a way to determine levels of detail.

Goal and detail are questions that we need to deal with as instructors. The Cokely (1992) and Colonomos (1992) models each provide us with ways of understanding the interpreting process. However, when we use either of these models, we still need some way to progress from basic skills to a full-blown successful interpretation.

Gish's goal-to-detail and detail-to-goal teaching approach (2001, 1986) meshes with the mapping we use. Her approach offers structure and hands-on strategies for teachers of interpreting skills. She begins by having students analyze the goal of a text, which she describes as "the purpose of the speech or the impact that the speaker wants to have on the audience" (Gish 1996, 4). She often expresses this goal with a verb that describes the presenter's intent: to entertain an audience, to persuade, and so on. Understanding the goal requires that students understand the context, registers, and styles of the source text. Once the goal of the text is determined, students analyze the source for its main objectives. Students can then identify the subobjectives of each main objective. Finally, students analyze at the level of individual proposition units. Some students may be ready to analyze a text only for the main objectives; others may be ready to analyze for the minutest details of the subobjectives. Regardless of the skill level that students bring to the task, they are able to experience success at their level. This helps them scaffold their learning, growing from where they are to where they need to be.

Our teaching approach is based on similar concepts, providing students with a visual structure for representing their understanding of a text. For some students, the random-concept-mapping activity may be the first step in enhancing comprehension of a source text. For other students, the use of drawings and pictures may be an essential step for them in order to escape the glossing rut into which they have fallen. For others still, the minute mapping of specific salient linguistic features may be the way to progress from inadequate to adequate to eloquent lexical choices. By having students make a random concept map, we are able to see what goal(s) they have understood from the source and what topics and subtopics, as well as details (or in Gish's terms, main objectives, subobjectives, and units) they have retained. Our next step, the linear, or sequential, map, allows us to see if they are able to reconstruct the source in a logical way—not necessarily in the exact sequence of the source but in a sequence that makes sense or that would be more effective in a target translation.

When applying our approach, we asked students to prepare a written translation using the class map. This was our final objective for this activity in this class. However, if a teacher has a different objective for the translation activity, additional follow-up activities could be added. The needs of each group of students will determine the subsequent activities selected by the teacher. Our discourse mapping, like Gish's goal-to-detail and detail-to-goal approach, offers a structure for students to experience success as they grow in their interpreting skills.

Assessing Student Work

Working from various maps of student work, we can often pinpoint patterns in their analysis and translations. By making a linear map of each student's translation, we are able to see which level of detail, subgoals, and major goals the student has included in the translation. The map provides an effective means of identifying patterns. Some students may have all the major themes but provide only one detail for each. Other students may have only one theme but provide an inordinate number of details. A third student may have missed one theme and included details from other themes, resulting in a confused and confusing translation.

When the instructors have made their own linguistic maps of the source, it is easier for them to find the language patterns. For example, we may discover that a linear map of a student's translation is missing the dialogue or, more likely, confuses which dialogue is associated with which character. At those points in the linear or sequential map where this confusion is evident, we can look at the source to find the salient linguistic features that may have resulted in the confusion. We may find that each time the translation shows confusion, the source (in this case, the signer) used naming strategies for "given" pronoun references: eye gaze, chin point, and head tilt, for instance, but not indexing, body shift, or renaming the referent. These naming strategies are commonly used for new referents in a text and are commonly taught in ASL classes. However, when they are missing, students are not aware of the omission; they may not know or may not have confidence in strategies that are more subtle, less visually salient, and (unfortunately for us) more common in everyday discourse.

Assessing Overall Content and Context

We assessed effectiveness of the sequential mapping activity using mapping strategies of our own. We developed our own linear map of the source in order to have a template from which to work. We were then able to assess the adequacy of the class-generated map, comparing the major topics and level of detail. In other courses, an instructor could ask each student to generate a sequential map, then assess the adequacy of each student's map. Or, if the instructor preferred to encourage more independent learning, the students could compare their own maps to the teacher's and to each other's. The map we have provided in figure 3 is partial, focusing on only some of the aspects we discuss related to evaluation.

Next we prepared a linear or sequential map based on each student's translation.[4] These maps included the essential points each

---

4. For this activity, we did not have the students create their own maps from their own translations. However, such an exercise can be very helpful as students assess their own work and the work of their peers.

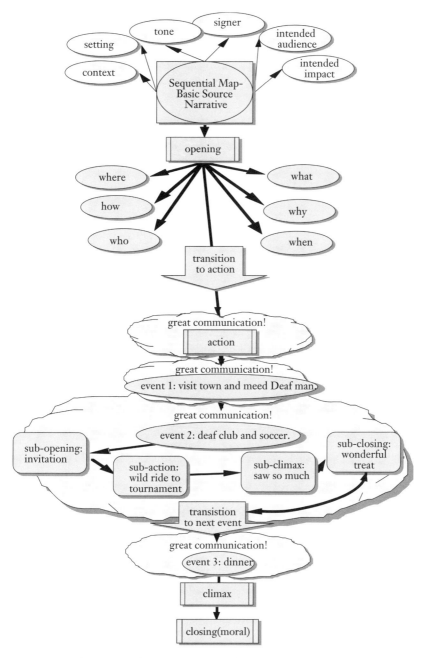

Figure 3. Teacher's map of source content and context

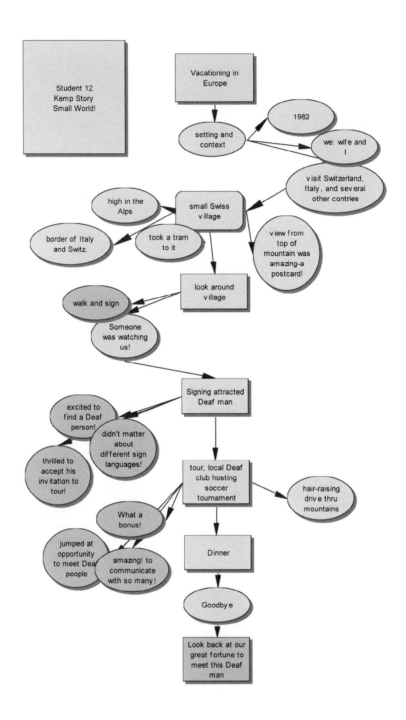

Student 12
Kemp Story
Small World!

Vacationing in Europe

setting and context

1982

we: wife and I

visit Switzerland, Italy, and several other contries

high in the Alps

small Swiss village

border of Italy and Switz.

took a tram to it

view from top of mountain was amazing-a postcard!

look around village

walk and sign

Someone was watching us!

Signing attracted Deaf man

excited to find a Deaf person!

didn't matter about different sign languages!

thrilled to accept his invitation to tour!

tour, local Deaf club hosting soccer tournament

hair-raising drive thru mountains

What a bonus!

jumped at opportunity to meet Deaf people

amazing! to communicate with so many!

Dinner

Goodbye

Look back at our great fortune to meet this Deaf man

Figure 4. Linear map 1

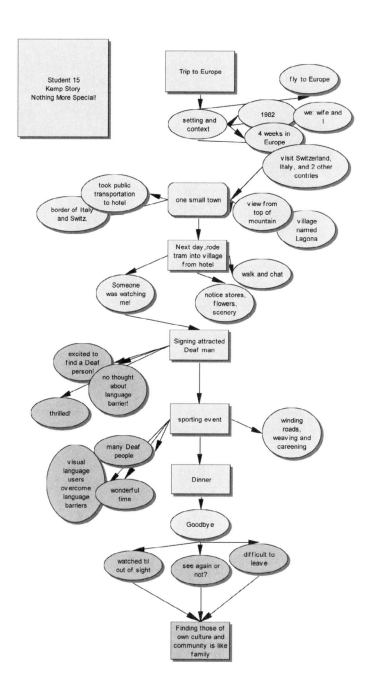

Figure 5. Linear map 2

translation included. See figures 4 and 5, which are based on two student translations.

Student A and student B had a similar number of events in the action areas, although each had some different details. Both repeatedly included the concept of enjoyment at the communication. And both included the ride through the mountains. Each also grouped some ideas differently, and each provided his or her own sense of the gist by adding a different title, but the similarity of the maps reflects the similarity of the translations and their adequacy in providing the content and context.

One student's linear map (figure 6) revealed that the idea of a gondola or tram ride up the mountain at one point in the source text was missing. This idea recurs late in the closing structure of the original and is a detail that adds eloquence to the story. Yet the deletion of the concept of "tram" does not irrevocably change the overall meaning of this student's translation, and the sense and tone of the source text are clearly reflected throughout. With this information, we can provide feedback to the student not only about what might have been missed but also about how significant it was in the source text and, most important, why it was significant.

Using our own map as a template, we were able to assess the adequacy of each student's translation in terms of content and context.

Assessing Target Form

We also used mapping to assess the resulting linguistic form of the students' translations. We chose specific areas of the original text and compared them to the translations. Our goal was to compare the linguistic forms used in the original text with the linguistic forms produced in the translations. Our expected outcome for the translation was that they be native-sounding written English texts with an eloquence similar to that of the original. Our mapping of the salient linguistic features in both the original and the translations provided an understanding of what made the original a story rather than a string of sentences and also identified what the

Figure 6. Linear map 3

69

students produced in their English translations of these features. We had no preconceived ideas of which English words or features needed to appear; we only expected that it read like a written English story prepared for a similar audience. We chose the areas of salient linguistic features in the source based on our experience and knowledge of problem areas for interpreters. Specifically, we wanted to explore the use of salient English features to produce a dynamically equivalent translation (see figure 7).

Having identified sections of the text that we predicted would pose challenges for the students, we compared how these sections were expressed in the translations. For this text, we analyzed and compared several areas, including the opening and closing of the text, topic and subtopic transitions, use of detail, adjectives, adverbs, sentence structure, and overall tone of the text. In the next section we discuss some of our findings from these comparisons.

The Bumpy Road—Complex Linguistic Features

One area we identified in the source was an elegant section of ASL text using classifiers and repetition; such a construction is often a challenge for interpreters. Given the ASL sentence VEHICLE:CL up and down ++++, we can compare the sentences and word choice in the English translations. Knowing that English uses adverbs, adjectives, and idioms to produce similar eloquence in English stories and does not serially repeat the verb itself, we can assess student skill in translation by looking for these salient English features. Thus, a translation such as "The car went up and down, bump, bump, bump," can be identified as less than adequate because it does not include adjectives, adverbs, or idioms and it does include a serial repetition of the verb. It is (as we already know) what is often labeled "glossing"—a semilinguistic equivalence. Although such an equivalence may be the goal in some environments, in most settings it is not. Rather, a dynamic equivalence, evoking the sense and feel of the passengers in the vehicle, is the more usual goal of story translation.

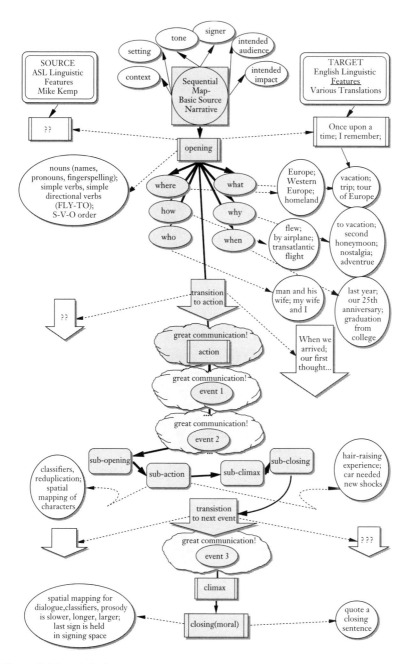

Figure 7. Linguistic features map

When we find sentences such as "It was a hair-raising experience but we managed to make it to and from in one piece!" (Student 11) or "We rode in his car, over winding roads, weaving and careening" (Student 15), we can state with confidence that the translation at this point has achieved a dynamic equivalence. The use of the idiom "hair-raising," along with an exclamation point to indicate the emphasis of the reduplication (++++) in the ASL text, all result in the English reader's sense of the ride. Of course, as a linguistic equivalent it is a dismal failure; from this translation, no audience would learn that ASL uses reduplication for emphasis. As a dynamic equivalent, however, it is a roaring success. Again, equivalence is relative, but in such a case, we believe a dynamic rather than a linguistic equivalence is most often the goal.

Meeting a Deaf Person—Culturally Rich Information

Another section we identified as challenging in the source text was the narrator's telling of a chance meeting with a Deaf man (while the narrator was on vacation in Europe). This is the essence of the story, the reason the narrator is describing his European vacation with his wife. The point of the story is not to tell about visiting historical sites or the beauty of the Alps. The point is that in a tiny little Austrian town, so very far away from home, an American Deaf couple met a local Deaf man and had a wonderful experience. The following gloss approximates the narrator's signs:

> WIFE, ME . . . CHAT+++, SIGN, WALK-along WALK++HAPPEN
> (someone to the left) LOOK-AT ME ME FEEL SOMETHING,
> (someone to the left) LOOK-AT ME INDEX MEET-ME, DEAF?
> TWO-OF-YOU, DEAF? WIFE AND ME, LOOK-AT-EACH-OTHER
> . . . FINE!

In this brief section lies the point of the story, and it is much more than simply meeting a Deaf man. When reviewing the student translations, we realized that many of them had actually captured the spirit of this narration:

- "Here, clear across the world was someone like us!" (Student 12)
- "Another Deaf person!" (Student 13)
- "Imagine our delight of running into someone who was deaf!" (Student 14)
- "I was stunned and at the same time, elated to meet a deaf person in this part of the country!" (Student 4)
- "My wife and I looked at each other and we knew this was a once-in-a-lifetime opportunity." (Student 2)

The word choices these students made reflect the linguistic complexity of the source text. The narrator does not mean "fine" with that one sign; he means to convey how thrilling it was to meet a Deaf person so far away from home, how excited he was to find a kindred spirit, how he knew the day was going to be a good one. Much information is conveyed in the sign FINE and in the facial expressions that appear in the source text; even more, however, is implied, and by allowing students to practice translating the source text, we have given them the time to reflect on the importance of these few signs.

STUDENT THOUGHTS ON THE TRANSLATION EXERCISE

To follow through with our beliefs about informing students of the expectations for a given activity (discussed above under "Specific Objectives for an Activity"), we asked for feedback when this translation exercise had been completed. Because it is important for instructors to appreciate translation from the point of view of the students, we are sharing some of their comments here, even though some of them are a bit long.

One of the themes of the student comments was the luxury of having time to think about the work. These comments certainly support our belief that practicing specific skills within the entire process is important, despite the opposing view that such exercises are not doable in the "real world." Students obviously saw the value of such a specific activity,[5] as shown by the following comments:

- "The translator has the ability to take the time they need to think about the source content and its goals, themes, and objectives." (Student 5)
- "Completing the translation shows how competent they [interpreters] are in the L2 [their second language] outside of any time constraints." (Student 8)
- "Provides a safe and controlled environment." (Student 3)
- "By giving the [interpreter] time to process, analyze, internalize, and retrieve data they can revisit the material without feeling the pressure (or need) to compete with anyone but him/herself." (Student 7)
- "When we have interpretations produced in real time, it can be difficult to identify the source of miscues." (Student 6)
- "I think one of the main goals of using translations for me will be to put all of these things together so they become an automatic part of my interpreting process." (Student 9)

Students also recognized another important benefit of this translation activity and the maps it included. When we introduced the random concept map, we told the students why we wanted to use drawings and pictures for the map rather than words or glosses. There was some discussion about this choice, and some students seemed reluctant to use pictures but agreed to try for this activity. Their comments indicate they came to see the value in such an approach.

- "If in the map we use pictures rather than words (signed or spoken) we may be more open to a wider vocabulary selection for our interpretation. (I am finding the use of pictures a personal chal-

---

5. We want to thank students in Project TIEM (Teaching Interpreting Educators and Mentors) Online Master Mentor program for their participation in this activity and for their reflective comments. Individual comments remain anonymous. We have identified them as "Student 1," "Student 2," and so on, so the reader can note the numerous responses we include.

lenge . . . and so I plan to do this kind of mapping to improve my own skills.)" (Student 6)

- "[Creating a map without words allows interpreters] to step away from the form of both the source language and the target language and think abstractly or conceptually . . . to create a clearer message . . . with fewer source language intrusions because they [interpreters] . . . truly dissect the message." (Student 5)
- "I do believe that it will allow me to have more optimal choices in future interpreting assignments by training my brain to look at the concepts visually; it frees me up from the textual level." (Student 10)

Finally, some students commented on goals and objectives that we had not made explicit for this activity; they are definitely worth reporting here and certainly need no additional discussion on our part:

- "The moment it started to make sense for me was when we went off on our own, made a translation from the map we drew (as a group) and then came back and compared our work. . . . The power of that process hit home for me when [Student 6] and [Student 8] talked about the comparison of their work. They both noted that even though their maps looked the same visually . . . their word choices, writing styles and overall compositions were very different. This only emphasizes the fact that there are many options for a successful interpretation and working with translations is one of the best ways to not only understand that, but discover what those options are." (Student 1)
- "Group brainstorming and mapping activities are wonderful opportunities for interpreters to use their L2 to discuss the L2 source text." (Student 8)
- "The translation can be used to look at specific skills on whether the 'big picture' was included: the goal and theme along with transitions, vocabulary choices, grammar of the target language, register, affect, cultural mediation, world view, etc. . . . Looking at the product, the translation, helps [interpreters] to look at the product more objectively." (Student 2)

- "As we go from viewing an ASL story to mapping out the story and then doing a translation and a retelling, we will learn more about one's comprehension of 'ASL' - Accuracy in content, Social appropriateness, Linguistic accuracy. Areas of focus or areas needing improvement can 'easily' be discovered." (Student 4)

Conclusion

It seems fair to say that translation is a valuable skill for interpreters who work between English and ASL. We have offered an in-depth look at one step in the discourse mapping process, the step that focuses on translation. The step began with creating a group random concept map, then a sequential map. Students then prepared their own translations, after which they returned to the larger group to compare and contrast their written work. When the activity was completed, the instructors created two separate linear maps, one from the students' translations and used to assess the equivalence of content and context, and one based on the linguistic complexity of the source and used to assess the equivalence of the English translations. Finally, students were asked to write their thoughts on the entire activity. Keeping in mind that these students were already working professionals, their comments offer us insight into the value of using discourse mapping to provide focused translation activities that are essential to the development of strong interpreting skills.

References

Cokely, D. 1992. *Interpretation: A sociolinguistic model.* Sign language dissertation series. Silver Spring, Md.: Linstok Press.

Colonomos, B. 1992. *Processes in interpreting and transliterating: Making them work for you.* Videotape. Westminster, Colo.: Front Range Community College.

Davis, J. E. 2000. Translation techniques in interpreter education. In *Innovative practices for teaching sign language interpreters,* ed. C. B. Roy, 109–31. Washington, D.C.: Gallaudet University Press.

Gish, S. 1986. Goal-to-detail and detail-to-goal. In *New dimensions in interpreter education: Task analysis—Theory and application. Proceedings of the 5th national convention, Conference of Interpreter Trainers*, ed. M. L. McIntire. Fremont, Calif.: Ohlone College.

———. 1996. Expectations of student interpreters: An emphasis on quality and control. *Conference of Interpreter Trainers News* 16 (2):4–5.

———. 2001. Lecture: Master Mentor Program, Project TIEM Online.

Kemp, M. No date. See now, never see again. In *ASL storytime*. Gallaudet University, School of Communication, vol. 2, story 6.

Larson, M. 1984. *Meaning-based translation: A guide to cross-language equivalence*. Lanham, Md.: University Press of America.

Nida, E. A. 1953. Selective listening. *Language Learning* 4 (3):92–101.

Seleskovitch, D. 1978. *Interpreting for international conferences: Problems of language and communication*. Silver Spring, Md.: RID Publications.

Wadensjö, C. 1998. *Interpreting as interaction*. New York: Longman.

Winston, E. A., and C. Monikowski. 2000. Discourse mapping: Developing textual coherence skills in interpreters. In *Innovative practices for teaching sign language interpreters*, ed. C. B. Roy, 15–66. Washington, D.C.: Gallaudet University Press.

LAURIE SWABEY

Beyond He Said, She Said: The Challenge of Referring Expressions for Interpreting Students

REFERRING EXPRESSIONS are an integral part of language and are present in every discourse that students interpret. In a sentence such as "The woman next door gave the green book to my son's friend," referring forms such as "the woman next door" and "the green book" are descriptive. However, the same meaning in context could be conveyed by the sentence, "She gave it to him." In this version, the pronominal forms *she*, *it*, and *him* are based on previous information that would have to be known to the listener in order for the sentence to be understood.

Thus pronouns, more than other words, depend greatly on their context for their meaning. For instance, the pronoun *it* is constrained only by the fact that its referent must be singular and inanimate; beyond that, many meanings are possible. However, in conversations we regularly understand sentences such as "She showed it to him" or "That doesn't tell her how it is." Even though pronouns such as these have the potential to cause ambiguities, in context listeners usually understand the intended referent without confusion (Halmari 1996).

However, most second-language learners have an easier time producing and comprehending full noun phrases (the teacher, my boyfriend's mother, doctor, my school) than other, less explicit referring expressions such as pronouns or referential shifting. Thus, although interpreting students may be able to understand the sign TEACHER in an American Sign Language (ASL) text, they may be less confident in their ability to track the other forms that are used to refer to the actions or thoughts of this teacher. This observation is supported by Taylor (2002) who reports that a common error for interpreters is "to omit information about referents in their interpretations, particularly when more than one character or object is referenced in the same sentence or when the signer switches quickly between constructed dialogue (speaking as the characters) and narrator mode (speaking directly to the audience)."

Many interpreting students produce interpretations before they have had the opportunity to develop sufficient competency and fluency in ASL. When faced with the complexities of the interpreting task, they tend to rely on their knowledge of referencing in English. As is typical for second-language learners, they overlay the knowledge and strategies that they use in their first language on the language they are acquiring. This strategy is ineffective and results in poor interpretations and student frustration.

Students need to keep in mind that referencing in ASL is much more complex than learning a pronominal system and then figuring out how and when to alternate between a full noun phrase (such as "the teacher") and a pronoun (she). The linguistic resources available in ASL, including the use of both hands, eye gaze, facial expression, torso/head movement, and space around the signer, allow fluent signers to refer to entities in multiple ways, both simultaneously and sequentially. As they begin interpreting, students face the complex task of having to track several types of information about reference simultaneously.

The teaching and learning approach described in this chapter involves students in developing an understanding of how, when, and why specific forms of reference are used in ASL and in English. This approach is based on observation, analysis, and application. In this way, students develop more effective strategies for using and comprehending referring forms; a more specific framework for analyzing their use of referring expressions in their own work and discussing that use with peers; and, over time, more facility with referring expressions, which leads to the ability to produce interpretations that are more fluent and accurate.

BACKGROUND ON REFERENCE FOR INTERPRETING STUDENTS

One of the aspects of reference that students find useful is the distinction between given and new information. New information is that which the speaker assumes to be introducing to the addressee or reactivating in the addressee's mind. In contrast, given information is the knowledge that the speaker assumes to be in the consciousness of the listener at the time of the utterance (Chafe 1976). In all languages, information that is given and that the speaker assumes to be in focus can by conveyed with forms that have the least phonetic content, such as pronouns or zero pronominals (Gundel, Hedberg, and Zacharski 1993). One of the most important effects of this given-versus-new distinction is that "given information is conveyed in a weaker and more attenuated manner than new information" (Chafe 1976, 1980). For all the languages studied to date, these forms, such as pronouns, which can be used to refer only to entities with a high degree of givenness, are predicted to be the hardest for non-native users to comprehend (Gundel, Hedberg, and Zacharski 1993).

It is not surprising, then, that interpreting students often struggle with accurately comprehending reference, specifically when the referents are in focus or have a high degree of givenness. For the majority of interpreting students who learned ASL as adults, forms that can be used only when the referent is in focus are usually the most difficult for them to understand in ASL. Although students follow explicit referents (the full noun phrase or a stressed point to a referent that was recently established), they often don't follow more subtle references to entities that are in focus, including those that might involve only a change in eye gaze.

Another useful framework for helping students understand the use of reference in discourse involves the following four factors, which influence how speakers choose to refer to an entity and what these choices signal to the listener (Ariel 1988).

1. Distance. If an entity has not been mentioned for several sentences, it is likely that the entity is not very salient in the mind of the hearer, and thus the speaker needs to provide a more explicit reference. Thus, the greater the distance, the less likely that a pronoun or other form used only for in-focus referents would be used.
2. Competition. This relates to the number of possible entities that could be the intended referent. For instance, in English, we have one singular subject pronoun that can be used to refer to a male: *he*. In an explanation in English that refers to two males, it may be ambiguous for a speaker to use the unstressed pronoun *he* consistently to refer to both males. In ASL when both males are in focus, an index to different locations could be used. Thus the resources a language has for expressing pronouns will influence the options available to the speaker.
3. Saliency. When the entity is part of the topic, it is more salient than if the entity is a nontopic.
4. Unity. Entities that are contained within the same frame are more salient than entities from a previous frame.

Again, entities that are salient and central to the current talk (i.e., that are in focus) can be referred to with more attenuated forms of expression than can entities that are less salient. Speakers mark those entities that bring up a new topic or are not central to the immediate focus of the discourse by the use of a more explicit referring form (i.e., a full noun phrase such as *the new patient* instead of the pronoun *she*).

The Cooperative Principle (Grice 1975) and Relevance Theory (Sperber and Wilson 1986, 1995) also shed light on how interlocutors understand referring expressions. According to the cooperative principle, cooperative speakers are not intentionally vague about reference and generally will not use a pronoun if it is likely to be misunderstood. As a result, listeners who are fluent language users do not consider every possible interpretation of a referent. Similarly, in a sentence in which a pronoun could refer to more than one entity, relevance theory predicts that the listener will choose the most easily understood interpretation that makes sense in the given context.

However, without a basic understanding of these principles, students may exhibit insecurity about how much they can rely on sense-making in their second language. For example, when working from ASL to English, if they don't see the referent in an overt, explicit form, some interpreting students feel they can't interpret it. They also may focus on looking for exact consistency in terms of spatial location, whereas context and focus can be more important. Devoting mental energy to worrying about seeing a specific overt referential form, as opposed to focusing on meaning and sense-making, is not a productive strategy for students.

Interpreting students have often not considered how effortlessly they understand various referring forms in their native language. Students who are native speakers of English can generally observe that in most of their interactions with other native speakers, they usually have little difficulty understanding the use of forms (such as *it, that, he, they, those*) that can be used to refer only to in-focus referents. Similarly, native ASL users have little trouble following rapid changes in referents that are in focus.

As will be described in the application section of this chapter, it is useful to do some classroom analysis of recorded interactions, both in ASL and in English. By having students consciously observe referring forms in both English and ASL and by guiding them through an analysis of the examples they collect, teachers help students more deeply internalize that understanding pronouns and other referring forms is not just a matter of decoding linguistic forms but is, more importantly, an inferential process.

The next section will look at some of the ways ASL refers to entities that are in focus as well as ways ASL and English differ in this regard.

Referring to In-Focus Entities in ASL

As stated earlier, students have the least trouble with comprehending and producing full noun phrases such as *that new teacher* and *the final paper*. Although full noun phrases such as these can be used to refer to entities that are in focus, ASL signers often choose to use forms that have a more restricted use and can be used only when the referent is in focus. As stated in the previous section, these are the forms that non-native speakers find most difficult. Even if students can understand and use these forms conversationally, they often find, when interpreting from English to ASL, that the source language influences their choices in the target language. For example, students sometimes think that if a pronoun such as *he* is used in English, an appropriate interpretation into ASL would be what they consider an equivalent form—an index to the appropriate location. However, depending on context, ASL has several options for referring to an in-focus referent, and one of these options might be more appropriate for the interpreter to choose. The options include using constructed action, a classifier predicate, "zero," meaning no use of a pronoun with a plain verb if the referent is clear in context; or incorporating the subject or object into the verb. A common pattern observed in ASL narratives is that after ASL storytellers introduce a particular referent, they immediately bring it into focus and then often interact with it as if it were present. This was not the approach of English speakers telling the same story (Swabey 2002).

When working from ASL to English, it is common for students to see rapid shifts between perspectives and referents and the simultaneous portrayal of more than one referent, as well as the simultaneous portrayal of the narrator perspective and the character perspective. Interpreting students, therefore, when working from ASL to English, may see two entities referred to at the same time, thus requiring them to track referents in a different way than they do in English. In their English-to-ASL work, they tend to forgo this type of simultaneity that a visual-spatial language allows, relying more on linear, English-like constructions. This issue of simultaneity is one that causes difficulty for students in both their ASL-to-English work and their English-to-ASL work and contributes to the nonfluent nature of their interpretations. This difficulty is described, with examples, in the following section.

In descriptions of role shifting, it has often been stated that the signer "takes on" the role of a specific character. However, Liddell (1998) provides a more accurate description based on the blending of two spaces. One of the spaces is what Liddell calls real space, which consists of the signer and the environment around him or her. The other space, in the case of the examples I will use here, is the story space. In the examples below, which consist of narrative retellings of "The Frog Story," the story space is the *signer's conception* of the story. (It is not the story itself.) In a grounded blend, these two spaces are combined, and the signer simultaneously portrays both the character from the story and his or her own narration (Liddell 1998). Liddell states that "knowing which mental space is active, as well as its spatial structure, is not only crucial to making referential determinations but is also crucial to a full understanding of all that the signer is expressing" (1998, 664).

I will give two examples of the use of grounded blended space from ASL narrative retellings by Deaf native signers of a line-drawn story, commonly referred to as "The Frog Story" (Mayer 1969). The first example occurred during the narration of the part of the story illustrated in figure 1 (Mayer 1969).

In his rendition of the story, a signer indicates the character of the boy by using the upper half of his body to portray the actions, attitudes, and emotions of that character. He uses both his own hands as the hands of the boy grabbing on to what the boy thinks are branches. (Unbeknownst to the boy, they are the antlers of a deer behind the bush.) At this point, the signer is using the story space. Next, however, the signer uses blended space as he adds narration. He does this by continuing to hold on to the branch/antler with his left hand and using his right hand to articulate the sign YELL. In this instance, the signer is simultaneously portraying the action of the boy and narrating the story. One of the English speakers used the following sentence for this same portion of the

Figure 1.

story: *The boy held on to some bushes for security as he called out for his frog.*

In another ASL example, the narrator conveys that the boy in the story ducks down as he is running away from an owl that is swooping down on him. The signer uses blended space again to convey this portion of the story. She bends over at the waist with her head and shoulders down, as though she is ducking down from something that is after her. However, her legs are not portraying the action of the boy running. She uses the sign RUN, as the narrator, to report the boy's action. In this way she uses her upper body to show the boy's upper body and, as narrator, uses the sign RUN to report the character's movement. One of the English speakers chose the following sentence for this section of the story: *He ducked down as he ran to get away.*

For these sections of the story, the English speakers usually used the noun phrase *the boy* and the pronoun *he*, but the ASL signers did not. In terms of the Givenness Hierarchy, the referent would need to be in focus in order to use constructed action without first specifically naming the referent (Gundel et al. 1993). In both of the above examples, this was the case.

During the narration related to the picture in figure 2, the ASL storyteller conveys that the boy is sleeping and knows nothing about the frog escaping. In his rendition, the signer uses his right hand to indicate the boy's hand holding on to his bedcovers. He leans his head and torso back and toward the left and closes his eyes to indicate that the boy is sleeping. The nonmanual marker ('th') and the sign articulated with the left hand (KNOW-NOTHING) indicate the narrator's perspective that the boy knew nothing about the escape of his frog. Thus the signer uses his mouth and left hand to narrate the story while simultaneously using his right hand, eyes, and torso to portray the sleeping boy. Identifying examples when signers convey a dual perspective—the narrator's point of view and the character's point of view—may help students solidify some of the differences between referring to entities in ASL and English.

The final example comes from the point in the story when the boy scoops up his frog to carry him home. In the ASL retellings, it was typical for signers to scoop up the frog (already in focus) in their hand. One signer, after holding the frog in his right hand and reacting to it, needed to continue the story with his dominant (right) hand. Instead of "dropping the frog" in order to continue

Figure 2.

signing with both hands (as students understandably might do), he seamlessly transferred the frog to his left hand and continued the story with his right hand. After another sentence, the nondominant hand turned over to produce the sign WALK. However, at this point the frog was no longer in focus.

In retelling this same event, another signer transferred the frog from the palm of the right hand to the palm of the left hand. He used his right hand to produce THANK-YOU, conveying his gratitude for the gift of the frog (which he maintained in focus with his left hand). He then produced the sign WALK. He retained the movement of the sign WALK with both hands but maintained the slightly cupped handshape with his left hand to represent the boy's hand holding the frog while his right hand used the conventional handshape for WALK. He kept the frog in focus by maintaining this handshape. When he signed KEEP, his right hand again used the normal parameters for the sign while his left hand (the base) remained slightly cupped, holding the frog. In this way, the signer maintained the in-focus status of the referents *frog* and *boy* while integrating the action sequences of holding, thanking, walking, and keeping.

As stated earlier, students have the least trouble with comprehending and producing full noun phrases such as *the little boy* and *his dog*. However, in the ASL examples given above, after a referent is introduced, the signers choose ways to express information about the referent other than by the use of overt pronouns or explicit noun phrases. Although they may understand the use of blended space well in conversational interactions, many interpreting students are weak at incorporating it in their interpretations. Furthermore, students sometimes assume that repetition of a noun or a pronoun adds to the clarity of their interpretations. By understanding how repetition is used in ASL discourse and in English discourse, students can make better decisions about using it in their interpreting work.

Another common, although less complex, frustration of interpreting students when they work from ASL to English is the incorrect perception that they have "missed" the referent. For example, this sometimes occurs in interpretations when students forget that, unlike English, ASL plain verbs do not require overt subjects if the topic, which is usually the subject, is clear from context (Lillo-Martin 1986). This use of zero pronoun is possible, although not required, when the referent is in focus. This is a brief example of something that students learn in an ASL class and have no difficulty understanding or producing conversationally but that can become less automatic when they move from language use to interpretation. It is also one of the aspects of reference that is easy for students to observe and discuss in terms of choices that ASL signers make related to use of the subject pronouns.

Interpreting students have generally developed the ability to use the basic principles of role shifting. However, their ability to use and comprehend rapid shifts in perspective is often not well developed. Students often have a better awareness of this after discussing a study by Morgan (1999) of British Sign Language (BSL) that can be applied to ASL.

Morgan describes what is commonly called role shifting as taking place in the shifted referential framework. He claims there are three referential frameworks that mark information differently: the shifted referential framework, the narrator framework, and the fixed referential framework.

The shifted referential framework is mainly used to describe dialogues, actions, and thoughts of protagonists, which he describes as being marked by eye-closes and nonmanual markers such as shoulder shifting or head tilts or both. Morgan contrasts this framework with the narrator framework, in which the signer's eye gaze is directed at the recipient. The signer uses this framework for the first mention of protagonists, comprehension checks, and narrative filling information. Finally, in the fixed referential framework, the signer's eye gaze is toward the hands. This framework is used for scene setting involving topographical space, the movements of referents by the use of pronominal classifiers, and pronominal points toward spatial loci. According to Morgan's study (1999) of two native BSL signers, there is often rapid interaction between the fixed referential framework and the shifted referential framework.

To put the above description in terms of the Givenness Hierarchy, it appears that if a referent is in focus, there is no need to rename the character, and rapid shifts in character can occur with shifts in eye gaze, shoulder shifting, facial expression, or a combination of these (Gundel et al. 1993).

Application

One of the difficulties that many interpreting students encounter is the requirement, at least in some programs, to interpret before they have adequately internalized the use of referring devices in ASL. Having students consecutively or simultaneously interpret before they have developed fluency beyond what is achieved in one or two years of college-level ASL courses can result in the fossilization of their ability to reference entities in ASL. Selinker (1972) describes fossilization as occurring when a second-language learner acquires an approximation of a particular aspect of a language, then uses that approximation on a regular basis, and because the approximation seems adequate in most situations, never develops true fluency.

The early introduction of interpreting skills encourages students to use referring expressions based on their knowledge of English because they are still too early in the process of learning ASL to have fully internalized how to use constructed action, constructed dialogue, zero pro, indicating verbs, blended space, and classifier constructions. Thus, they use a few basic strategies, such as repetition of the full noun phrase or pronoun, simple use of left and right space, the "listing convention," and an elementary form of referential shifting. Interpreting before they have developed sufficient competency with referring expressions pushes them to develop coping mechanisms instead of fluency.

In the next section two teaching-learning approaches aimed at developing students' knowledge of and facility with referring expressions are described. Because of the weakness of most interpreting students in the area of reference, we start with language analysis activities, not interpreting activities, thus allowing students to develop competency with referring expressions without the additional task of interpreting.

Observation and Documentation

Many students seem to have had very little exposure to observing and analyzing the languages they hear and see in their daily environment. Although students often do not display much eagerness in discussing definite and indefinite determiners or demonstrative and personal pronouns, they can become intrigued with collecting samples of referring expressions, recording them in a notebook or on tape, and discussing their examples in class. With their examples, they need to provide some context, as well as the utterance they found relevant. I use their examples as a springboard for teaching concepts related to reference.

The students I have taught using this approach have learned ASL as a second language as adults, so we begin with examples from English. The following are some examples of utterances students have contributed to the class discussion. I have not included contextual information, which is also used in the discussion.

- He told him he needed an MRI.
- He talked with him for almost thirty minutes.
- She was fed up with her because she wouldn't give her a referral to a specialist.
- That's not what she was referring to when she told you about it.
- Have you heard back from that woman who told you you couldn't send her those forms?
- Where did she get that and how long has it been here?
- How long will it take before he knows if he made it or not?
- If she gets it done in time, will you take her to her thing tonight?
- My friend just got divorced. She has a daughter and now she has to learn how to drive.

By spending a short amount of time considering the speakers, the context, and the referring form chosen by the speaker, students develop more awareness of English and how meaning is derived from pronouns that, out of context, can refer to an endless number of entities. Students see how little meaning their examples have when isolated. However, generally at the time the utterances were said, they made perfect sense to both the speaker and the hearer. This realization leads to a better understanding regarding the comprehension of referring expressions, to wit: focusing on the meaning and intent of speakers within the context is more important than focusing on individual lexical items. I also bring in recorded examples of rapid, conversational speech to illustrate how the phonetic content of pronouns can change. Consider "Didja see 'im?" (Did you see him?), "Diddy get 'em?" (Did he get them?), and "Teller" (Tell her). Students are often not aware how effortlessly they understand pronouns in their native language, even in rapid conversation.

Students are likewise asked to record instances in which a pronoun or other referent was used and misunderstood by the interlocutors and to note why they think it was misunderstood and how it was resolved.

Finally, we do some analysis of recorded talk and transcripts of recorded talk. This analysis is an excellent base for discussing concepts such as given and new information, particularly when identifying which entities are in focus. Referential choices can be examined according to the four factors defined by Ariel (1988), including distance, competition, saliency, and unity. Much can be gleaned from a very short section of a transcript; even focusing on just one factor (such as distance or competition) can lead to interesting analysis of the reasons a particular referent was chosen by a speaker.

Next, students are asked to bring in examples in ASL. This is a slower process, and usually the examples are fairly sparse and basic at the beginning. As students continue with the exercises in the next section, however, they become more adept at identifying referring forms and noting examples for class. Students are often very interested in the differences and similarities with English. Examples that generate the most discussion often involve those that use blended space and constructed action.

As with their English observations, students are asked to record misunderstandings they observe related to reference in ASL, along with why they think the referent was misunderstood and how the misunderstanding was negotiated or resolved. They also record instances in which they misunderstood a referring form, the reason they think the misunderstanding occurred, and what resolution, if any, was negotiated.

Videotaped examples in ASL are essential for analyzing and discussing examples of given and new information and how in-focus entities are referenced in ASL. Digital video allows students to view passages frame by frame, thus providing them the opportunity to see and analyze rapid shifts they might miss on VHS or in live interactions. Viewing examples on videotape often leads to the topic of assimilation, the influence of one segment on another segment so that they become more alike or identical. Students are often fascinated to find how PRO.1 can change, depending on what comes before it. For example, on one videotape, the signer began a sentence with PRO.1 ENTER. However, she did not use the citation form of PRO.1 with the index finger pointing to the center of the upper chest. Instead she used the same handshape as she would use for the sign ENTER, except with a slight bent. It was placed more to the right of the chest area, not in the center.

Another example illustrates how the noun can also change. In this case, the signer was talking about a boy waking up in the morning. Although the boy was already in focus and the signer had several options for referring to the boy, she chose to use the noun BOY, but she made the sign on the right side of her face, next to her eye, in the same location where she would immediately sign WAKE-UP. Her hand closed with the handshape for BOY and opened with the handshape for WAKE-UP. Students often have not considered that this type of assimilation may occur when the referent is in focus.

ANALYSIS OF MODEL LANGUAGE SAMPLES AND STUDENT LANGUAGE SAMPLES

The book *Frog, Where Are You?* (Mayer 1969) has been used as a stimulus for eliciting language samples in several cross-linguistic studies and well as studies of sign languages (Berman and Slobin 1994; Morgan 1999). It works well for teaching reference because it has three protagonists as well as various objects that require students to show more than one character or action simultaneously. The story line is not complex, however, and it is possible to collect samples of the same text from native signers and speakers so that students are exposed to a variety of possibilities, not just one correct way of producing a particular concept.

Preparation

Student Tapes

Students individually read the line-drawing book *Frog, Where Are You?*. Students should spend about ten minutes becoming familiar with the story, which they will retell in ASL. This is not meant to be a formal translation but a sample of each student's ability to spontaneously retell the story. Because there are no words, there is no English interference from the original text.

When students tell the story in ASL, they are not allowed to refer to the book. They are to tell the story from memory, incorporating as much detail as they comfortably can. Students should not worry about including every detail in the story, although as much information as possible is desirable. If students tell it and feel it isn't representative of their ASL work, they can tape it again during the same class period.

The tapes are not used immediately after they are made. Before they analyze their work, the students analyze the work of some native Deaf ASL signers.

ASL Language Models (Deaf Native Signers)

Following the same procedure as above, recruit at least three Deaf ASL signers who are comfortable being videotaped and enjoy storytelling. As above, they are to take about ten minutes to become familiar with the story and then to tell it comfortably without referring to the book. It is not crucial that every detail in the book be included; a natural flow to the story is more important than pausing to search for exactly the next scene. If possible, record the Deaf ASL models on digital videotape so that the shifts in reference can be analyzed in depth. Again, it is important for the storyteller not to refer to the book while telling the story.

English Language Models (Hearing Native Speakers)

Follow the same procedure as above, except with hearing people who like to tell stories and feel comfortable being videotaped. To be consistent with the students and Deaf storytellers, the English speakers should not hold or look at the book as they tell the story. Each student can be responsible for videotaping one English speaker (a nonsigner) and transcribing the tape. Alternately, the instructor can make at least three tapes (with transcriptions) for the class to use.

Classroom Work and Analysis

The first part of this activity consists of small groups of students analyzing the tapes made by the native ASL signers. I find that for video analysis, three seems to be the ideal group size. Students who have developed some facility with identifying in-focus referents are probably ready to work in small groups. Students who are not yet so adept may benefit from the instructor's demonstrating the process before working in small groups.

These *Frog Story* tapes tend to be very rich, and they can be used in a number of ways. First, the small group should watch the entire story. Depending on the group, the instructor can assign a certain segment of the story to analyze or allow the group to find examples anywhere in the story. The following questions can be used to stimulate analysis and discussion of the tapes in the small groups. These discussions should be conducted in ASL. Students should document their observations and discussions.

Who is the first character mentioned? Is the first mention different from the second mention and subsequent mentions of the character?

Who is the second character mentioned? What forms does the storyteller use to refer to the character in subsequent mentions?

How many times is pronominal indexing used to refer to each of the three main characters?

If the storyteller portrays an animal or creature being picked up and
held, how does the signer move on with the story? Is the animal
or creature "dropped"? Are animate entities (such as animals)
handled differently from inanimate objects?

Find at least one example in which the signer holds a referent with
one hand while showing some other type of information (action,
narration, etc.) with the other hand. Why is this done? What
happens with the hand that is "holding" the referent?

Find at least one example of blended space. Would you have
thought to use blended space in this manner to convey this concept? Why or why not?

Find at least three examples of the use of zero pro. How does this
signer's use of zero pro compare to your use of zero pro?

How often are the signs BOY, FROG, and DOG used? When are these
characters indicated by a pronoun, referential shift, eye gaze,
classifier predicate, or other reference tracking device?

Related to reference, what did you see in the model story that you
think you also incorporated into your rendition?

What have you seen in the model version that you would like to incorporate into the next version of your telling of the story? Why?

What was the most striking difference you found in comparing the
way the model signer referred to entities and the way you refer to
entities?

Students should repeat this activity with at least one other model
tape, preferably two.

Peer Analysis of Student Tapes

Ideally, students would transcribe portions of their ASL tapes. It is
often instructive to pick a short series of images from the original
book and ask them to transcribe the portion of their ASL rendition
that corresponds to the selected pictures

Again, students should work in groups of three. The group
should begin by viewing, without stopping, the tape to be analyzed

After that, the group should go through the tape again, analyzing the use of referring forms and answering the questions used for the model ASL tapes. These observations and examples should also be documented. After comparing and contrasting the student versions with the model ASL versions, each student should select at least one portion of the story (based on the original picture text) to retell and record. This version should represent what they have learned from analyzing the ASL texts, the small-group work, and the class discussions. Students should present their final rendition (on tape). Before presenting their tape in class, students also prepare a brief video in which they describe (in ASL) what changes they made related to referencing from their first rendition and why they made those changes. This tape can be used as preparation for a final discussion or can be part of the assessment of the project.

Finally, students analyze the renditions of native English speakers and, after analyzing the English tapes, compare the use of referencing in the English and ASL versions.

The above exercises have not focused on interpretation but instead have engaged students in developing more knowledge about referring expressions and an increased ability to understand and produce a broader range of referring forms. By not complicating this process with the addition of the interpreting task, students can devote their attention to language knowledge and proficiency, which ultimately benefits their interpreting work. After completing these activities, students work with other types of texts and eventually transfer the skills developed to consecutive interpreting.

Conclusion

Given the complexity of referencing and the different options speakers have for referring to entities in ASL and in English, it is not surprising that students often have difficulty incorporating referencing effectively in their interpretations. Although substantial research has been conducted in the area of reference in several disciplines, including philosophy, linguistics, and psychology, this work has not been applied extensively in the field of interpretation. Students benefit from having a broad understanding of the use of reference in language in general and in ASL and English in particular.

With this background, students can develop a more analytical, less arbitrary, and less emotional framework for analyzing and discussing their own work related to referring expressions. Equally important, providing students with some theoretical background on reference reinforces the importance of comprehending and transmitting meaning because it illustrates the limitations of basing interpretations primarily on linguistic form. Finally, the ability to more accurately comprehend and convey referring expressions allows interpreting students to move toward a higher level of accuracy, fluency, and confidence in their work.

REFERENCES

Ariel, M. 1988. Referring and accessibility. *Journal of Linguistics* 24:67–87.

Berman, R., and D. Slobin. 1994. *Relating events in narrative: Crosslinguistic developmental study*. Hillsdale, N.J.: Erlbaum.

Chafe, W. 1976. Givenness, contrastiveness, definiteness, subjects, topics and points of view. In *Subject and topic*, ed. C. Li, 27–56. New York: Academic Press.

———, ed. 1980. *The pear stories: Cognitive, cultural, and linguistic aspects of narrative production*. Norwood, N.J.: Ablex.

Grice, H. P. 1975. Logic and conversation. In *Syntax and semantics*, ed. P. Cole and J. L. Morgan, 41–58. New York: Academic Press.

———. 1989. *Studies in the way of words*. Cambridge, Mass.: Harvard University Press.

Gundel, J., N. Hedberg, and R. Zacharski. 1993. Cognitive status and the form of referring expressions in discourse. *Language* 69:274–307.

Halmari, H. 1996. On accessibility and coreference. In *Reference and referent accessibility*, ed. T. Freitheim and J. Gundel, 155–78. Pragmatics and Beyond New Series, vol. 38. Amsterdam: Benjamins.

Liddell, S. 1998. Grounded blends, gestures, and conceptual shifts. *Cognitive Linguistics* 9 (3):283–314.

Lillo-Martin, D. 1986. Two kinds of null arguments in American Sign Language. *Natural Language and Linguistic Theory* 4:415–44.

Mayer, M. 1969. *Frog, where are you?* New York: Dial.

Morgan, G. 1999. Event packaging in British Sign Language discourse. In *Storytelling and conversation: Discourse in deaf communities*, ed. E. Winston, 27–58. Washington, D.C.: Gallaudet University Press.

Selinker, L. 1972. Interlanguage. *IRAL* 10 (3):209–31.

Sperber, D., and D. Wilson. 1986. *Relevance: Communication and cognition.* Cambridge, Mass.: Harvard University Press.

———. 1995. *Relevance: Communication and cognition.* 2nd ed. Oxford, U.K.: Blackwell.

Swabey, L. 2002. The cognitive status, form and distribution of referring expressions in ASL and English narratives. Ph.D. diss., University of Minnesota.

Taylor, M. 2002. *Interpretation skills: American Sign Language and English.* Edmonton, Alberta, Canada: Interpreting Consolidated.

MELANIE METZGER

Interpreted Discourse: Learning and Recognizing What Interpreters Do in Interaction

INTERPRETERS' WORK is discourse. Although varying approaches to the study and pedagogy of interpretation exist, one cannot deny that the basic work that interpreters engage in on a daily basis is the comprehension and manipulation of discourse. In addition to the need for interpreters to study and gain control over such cognitive tools as information processing, memory, and decision making, interpreters must be able to recognize those aspects of discourse that pertain to its pragmatic function. Equally important, interpreters must be cognizant that their very presence changes the structure and flow of interaction (Roy 1989a, 2000a; Wadensjö 1992, 1998; Metzger 1995a, 1999; Angelleli 2001, 2003).

A growing body of research suggests that interpreters do far more than work as conduits between primary participants. Roy (1989a, 2000a) and Sanheim (2003) find that interpreters actually exhibit some control in interpreted interactions, through the management of turn-taking. Wadensjö (1992, 1998) finds that spoken language interpreters can be seen to engage in two basic acts when interpreting interaction: relaying and coordinating. Metzger (1995a, 1999) finds that interpreters generate their own turns while interpreting interaction and that these turns provide evidence of both of these functions: relaying and coordination, or interactional management. Angelleli (2001, 2003) finds that interpreters are far

100

more visible participants in medical interactions than was once thought to be the case, engaging in a variety of self-generated turns at talk. Research provides evidence of what occurs in practice in the field; it also provides a catalyst for adjusting interpreter education so that students are better prepared to work after graduation.

Toward this end, Metzger (2000) describes the importance of teaching interpreting students about the features of interactive discourse and the role that interpreters have been found to play when interpreting interaction (Metzger 2000). In that study, Metzger proposes that students should be able to do the following:

1. Recognize and identify features of interactive discourse
2. Understand interpreters' strategies for coping
3. Apply strategies for coping (Metzger, 85)

This chapter builds on this earlier work and focuses on teaching specific strategies in greater depth. Toward this end, this chapter will review the features of interactive discourse described in Metzger (2000), focus on one feature, source attribution, as a sample, and then propose a general approach for assisting students in the recognition and identification of each specific interactive discourse feature so that students can better employ them in their interpretations.

FEATURES OF INTERPRETED INTERACTION

By studying an interpreted English-American Sign Language (ASL) doctor-patient encounter (Metzger 1995a, 1999), an interpreted professor-student meeting (Roy 2000a), and several medical and social service interviews (Wadensjö 1998), numerous features of interpreted interaction have been identified, labeled, and described that can be used in teaching interpreters. These features include introductions, attention-getting strategies such as summonses, turn-taking and overlap, responses to questions directed to the interpreter, requests for clarification, relaying of pronominal reference, and source attribution. In this section, these strategies will be reviewed from a descriptive, empirical perspective. The remainder of this chapter will apply a prescriptive and pedagogical perspective to one strategy and suggest ways to apply this approach to the others.

FEATURES OF INTERACTIONAL MANAGEMENT

Introductions

When people gather for almost any type of interaction, introductions are the way that the interaction gets started. This is true in casual and information gatherings. The interaction may begin with a question about whether all the people present know one another. Similarly, in more formal or structured interactions, such as interviews or meetings, the interaction begins with some sort of introduction. This might be a brief opening to get the event started, or it might be a detailed and thorough introduction in which all participants have the opportunity to say their name and offer other identifying information about themselves, such as professional credentials and business or academic affiliation. The information included in introductions may well be culturally motivated. Further, when the interaction is interpreted, the interpreter may be introduced, and information regarding the unique qualities of interpreted interaction may be shared.

The introduction of the interpreter can be handled in any one of a variety of ways. For example, the interpreter can make the introduction or be introduced by one of the primary participants. However, because in an interpreted encounter the primary participants do not communicate using the same language, problems can arise with either of these options. If a primary participant introduces the interpreter, that participant may not describe the role of the interpreter or the interpreting process completely or correctly. Conversely, if the interpreter attempts a self-introduction, questions arise over which language to use first. These decisions reflect the difficulty of three-person interactions (Simmel 1950). That is, when the interpreter uses one of the languages, the other language user, if inexperienced regarding interpreted interaction, may feel left out or even confused. Moreover, signed-to-spoken language interpreters might attempt the introduction in a simultaneous manner (signing and speaking at the same time). This, too, can be problematic, leading to unclear or incomprehensible utterances in one language or the other (Metzger 1995a, 1999).

Descriptive research offers some insight regarding effective ways to manage interpreter introductions. Nevertheless, more research remains to be done that takes into account not only the effectiveness of the introduction on the subsequent interaction but also the impact of the decisions made on the primary participants in terms of their motivation and confidence in continuing the discourse. Students benefit from discussion, observation, and practice not only with these areas of introduction but also with the culturally motivated introductions commonly found in the settings in which they work.

Summonses

Every language has a means for getting the attention of others. For example, speakers of English might use a variety of address forms to gain other people's attention, including calling their name or title or title and name, as in, "Mr. Dawson, I have a question" or "Aunt Wendy, may I have some water?" Attention-getting devices in signed languages can be quite different, using indexing, a hand wave, or tapping another primary participant (Baker 1977; Baer 1991) or moving into the line of sight of the addressee (Mather 1990; FitzPatrick 1993; Chen 1993).

Students of interpretation not only need to know that these devices differ; they must also be aware of the fact that in monologic interaction, hearing-hearing or deaf-deaf interactions may not even require the use of an attention-getting strategy when interpreted interaction does. I have pointed out elsewhere (Metzger 1995a; 1999) that in an interpreted medical examination, a Deaf mother often must attend to the needs of her sick child. The hearing medical staff is not aware of whether she is looking when they begin to take a turn. In fact, with a hearing mother, all they need to do is speak; the sound of the voice will pull the hearing mother's attention away from her child and back to the interview. However, if the interpreter does not use a visual attention-getting device, then the Deaf mother has no way of knowing that she is missing information. Similarly, the Deaf mother might sign a question to the doctor. The doctor may be equally unaware of being addressed, and by whom, unless the interpreter makes this information, as well as the content of the question, clear.

In addition to learning about when to summon primary participants, interpreting students must learn how to summon them. Not all strategies are equally viable in a given setting. Although a tap on the arm of the Deaf mother might be appropriate in some settings, it might not in others. Moreover, interpreting with deaf children in hearing-mainstreamed classrooms requires repeated summonses for a variety of reasons, all of them important, but not equally important. A deaf student needs to know that nearby students are quietly discussing the current assignment in order to have an opportunity to participate or overhear the information. That student also needs to know if the teacher announces that the current task must be completed within three minutes. It is also necessary to summon the student when the teacher resumes the lecture. The interpreting student must be prepared to summon a student in a manner equal to the urgency of the source (see Mather 1994 for a discussion of signing on a level with and in alignment with deaf children in school).

Turn-Taking and Overlap

In every language, interlocutors must negotiate the taking, maintaining, and yielding of turns. Native users of a language know to attempt to gain the floor at a moment in which the discourse allows it (Sacks, Schegloff, and Jefferson 1974; Baker 1977). Primary participants may also have interactional goals that cause them to intentionally interrupt a speaker, give a turn to another primary participant, or overlap with a current speaker to show interest and rapport (Tannen 1984). The discursive strategies that speakers and signers use, and the motivation behind them, must be translated just as the content of utterances is translated, in search of equivalence.

Students of interpretation can also benefit from the recognition that in order to allow an interpreted interaction to continue, the interpreter must face frequent decisions about how to handle this negotiation of turns and overlap. In fact, in interpreted discourse, overlap is not only akin to the overlap that occurs in monolingual interaction; overlap occurs as a result of the lag between original utterances and relayings and possibly as a result of confusion about who has the floor and whether or not a pause signals the end of a turn or an interpreter's requesting clarification. The interpreter can do the following:

1. Stop one or both speakers
2. Continue to relay one person's utterance, remembering the second person's utterance and relaying it after the first has been completed
3. Disregard the overlap
4. Continue to relay one person's utterance and, when done, offer a turn to the other participant (or otherwise indicate the attempted turn) (Roy 2000a)

Students of interpretation must learn how to effectively incorporate these options into interpreted interactions. They must also learn what to expect and how to apply the options in different settings. For example, turn-taking takes very different forms depending on whether it takes place in a classroom, a courtroom, or a staff meeting. For a more in-depth discussion related to interpretation and turn-taking, see Roy (2000a).

Responses to Questions

Experienced consumers of interpreted interaction often understand the underlying notion that interpreters are not primary participants in the encounter. As a result, experienced consumers are not likely to engage an interpreter in conversation; at least they are less likely to do so unless their comments relate to the interpretation process itself. For example, a more experienced consumer might ask the interpreter to alter his or her location so that the interpretation is more accessible (visibly or audibly, depending on the languages involved). Conversely, a less experienced consumer is more likely to engage an interpreter in conversation related to topics not limited to the interpreting process. For example, such a consumer might ask an interpreter how to sign something in ASL if that is the language the consumer doesn't know (Metzger 1995a, 1999).

The fact that primary participants direct questions to interpreters is not particularly surprising. What is challenging, however, is to consider what sort of responses the interpreter can provide that facilitate their reason for being present. I have pointed out before (Metzger 1995a, 1999, 2000) that an interpreter has a range of possible responses, including the following:

1) Ignore the question and not respond
2) Provide a minimal response, not necessarily answering the question
3) Providing a lengthier explanation, either in response to the question itself or to explain the role of the interpreter.

In every situation in which a primary participant directs a question to an interpreter, the interpreter must make a decision about how to respond. This decision should be based on a combination of sociolinguistic, cultural, and situational factors that support interactional goals.

To teach students how to make such decisions, it is useful to address the considerations they face. For example, from a sociolinguistic perspective, a question is the first part of an adjacency pair, a two-part sequence in interactive discourse (Schegloff 1972, Schegloff and Sacks 1973). As such, a question requires a second part, or a response, in order for the discourse to unfold smoothly. With this in mind, it makes sense from a sociolinguistic perspective that at the very least, interpreters provide some sort of minimal response, even if one without content, so that the discourse may proceed. Students are better prepared for the real world of interpreting work if they have the opportunity to discuss, observe, and produce responses to questions.

Relayings

Requests for Clarification

Many interpretation theorists agree that interpreters cannot interpret until they comprehend what a speaker has uttered (Cokely 1992; Colonomos 1995; Gile 1995; Gish 1987; Seleskovitch 1998). This is a major rationale for assignment preparation. The more background information interpreters gather, the fewer questions they will have while working. Nevertheless, even the most professionally prepared interpreter cannot have so much background information that they have no need for additional information while on the job. As Gile (1995) points out, one of the resources available to an interpreter is the speaker. Students of interpretation must learn the appropriate ways and times to request clarification during interaction and how these ways and times might vary across a diversity of settings.

Relaying of Pronominal Reference

Primary participants use the first-person pronoun to refer to themselves. Interpreters generally interpret in first person. That is, the interpreter often uses first-person pronouns to refer to someone else, specifically, to the originator of the utterance being relayed. However, this is not always the case. In earlier work (Metzger 1995a, 1999) I found that in ASL-English interpretation, an interpreter uses first person to match the source most or all of the time when interpreting from ASL to English. The same interpreter does not always match the use of pronominals in English-to-ASL interpretations. The interpreter's use of first-person pronoun can be confusing to an inexperienced consumer. I found the English-speaking consumer asked the interpreter to clarify whom the first-person pronoun referred to.

Interpreters also sometimes omit pronominal reference, as when a primary participant says, "Tell her . . ." or "Ask him. . . ." All of these choices have implications regarding the process and effectiveness of the interpretation. For example, in the latter case, if a primary participant is being talked about without realizing it, the participant cannot respond to that indirect discourse. In the case of Deaf consumers, use of interpreters is quite frequent. Many Deaf consumers prefer that their hearing interlocutors communicate as directly as possible. Including such information is a way of providing interactional equivalence to consumers.

Source Attribution

In the interpretation of any interaction that involves more than two people, consumers will likely not know who the source of a particular utterance is unless the interpreter makes that information explicit. In fact, because interpreters themselves must often generate utterances (to stop a speaker who has overlapped or to summon the attention of a participant, for example), even in an interaction with two participants, the interpreter represents a third person capable of contributing to the discourse. Thus, in any interpreted encounter, consumers cannot be certain who is responsible for a particular utterance unless the interpreter attributes the source (either to herself or someone else). Source attribution is the focus of the remainder of this chapter and will be discussed in more depth below.

SOURCE ATTRIBUTION

As I have written elsewhere (Metzger 1995a, 1999), source attribution refers to an interpreter-generated utterance designed to indicate the source of a translated utterance. It might take a variety of forms, such as, "The doctor said . . . ," but the importance of source attribution is that without it, a primary participant may not know who is responsible for an utterance.

At first glance, it seems likely that interlocutors will know whose utterances are being relayed at any given moment. However, this is not necessarily the case. Certainly in small-group interaction, it is easy enough for interlocutors to become confused about whose utterance is being relayed because of the time lag between a primary party's utterance and the translation. That is, interlocutor A might take a turn at talk, followed by interlocutor B. Interlocutor A's utterance is being relayed during interlocutor B's turn. Yet participants relying on the interpretation may make the assumption that the translation happens nearly simultaneously, thus attributing to interlocutor B the relayed utterance of interlocutor A. Moreover, even in one-on-one encounters, interpreters generate their own utterances. This being the case, a primary participant can never be certain whether a given utterance by the interpreter is the interpreter's own or the relayed utterance of the other primary participant[1] (Metzger 1995a, 1999).

The significance of source attribution in simultaneous, interactive interpretation is underscored in a study comparing discourse genre and discourse mode (Metzger, Fleetwood, and Collins 2004). In this study, my analysis of interpreter-generated utterances (Metzger1995a, 1999) is compared with two additional cases of interpreted interaction. In the first case, a signed language interpreter is interpreting for a Deaf student in a hearing university classroom. In the second, a signed language interpreter is interpreting a videotaped panel interview between a Deaf, sighted moderator and a Deaf-Blind panelist. Perhaps not surprisingly, the study finds that source attribution occurs most frequently in the tactile mode. However, the difference is quite significant; the tactile interpretation includes 100 percent attribution of source; even when there is a prior naming by others of the next interlocutor to take a turn, the interpreter still identifies that next person. The authors conclude that the discourse mode provides impetus for making the source 100 percent clearly identified, meaning that a Deaf-Blind interlocutor will not use the same contextual information as a sighted one to determine the source of a given utterance. However, the authors propose that application of the same rigorous conveyance of

---

1. Some factors, such as context, may assist an interlocutor in making the correct determination. However, the relevant point here is that as long as there may be confusion about a given utterance, source attribution reduces the confusion.

source attribution in other discourse genres and modes might be desirable.[2]

SOURCE ATTRIBUTION IN ASL

In English-to-ASL interpretation, source attribution can take many forms. At least six types of source attribution are possible (Metzger, Fleetwood, and Collins 2004). They are based on the analysis of three cases of interpreted interaction. They include four single forms of attribution, each of which provides different information about the source: body shift, eye gaze, index-to-source, and name/description. These four can be combined to provide more explicit information about the source, as will be seen below.

Body Shift

Interpreters use body shifting as a visual strategy for distinguishing between speakers who are taking turns. Body shifting can consist of a slight adjusting of the location of the shoulders, torso, or head of the signer. Although there has not been an extensive study of body shifting as it occurs in interpreted discourse, studies (Metzger 1995a, 1999; Metzger, Fleetwood, and Collins 2004) have found that interpreters do utilize this shift, comparable to the kind of body shifting associated with constructed dialogue and constructed action in ASL (see Roy 1989b; Winston 1991, 1992; Metzger 1995b; Liddell and Metzger 1998), to distinguish between speaker turns. I have pointed out (Metzger 1995a, 1999) that this feature occurs so similarly to ASL noninterpreted discourse that it is as if the interpreter were reporting the dialogue of the primary participants who are actually present using the same discourse strategy that native signers use when describing past or imagined conversations in ASL narrative discourse. Body shifting as a sole strategy

---

2. As the authors note, further study is warranted to determine when and how source attribution clarifies understanding for primary participants or whether it is ever unnecessary or undesirable.

provides information to the observer about the fact that a change in speaker has occurred, but it does not provide information about the location of that speaker or the speaker's identity (such as name or appearance).

Eye Gaze

Looking at the source of an utterance being interpreted is a strategy interpreters use to identify whose utterance is being relayed (Metzger, Fleetwood, and Collins 2004). The interpreter's looking at the source gives the observer information about who is responsible for the content of the relayed utterance. It may also be useful for the interpreter, who can gain information by seeing the person taking a turn. Eye gaze alone, depending on the number of people in an interaction and the way they are situated in relation to one another, provides, at the very least, information about the location of the source. It may also provide information about a shift from one speaker to another. However, eye gaze alone may not be sufficient to identify the exact source of an utterance.

Index-to-Source

Index-to-source refers to a point of the index finger to the source of the utterance being relayed. This point might designate any of the primary participants, or even the interpreter for utterances that are interpreter-generated (see Fleetwood and Metzger 1990, Metzger 1995a, 1999). Pointing with the index finger can fulfill a number of grammatical and pragmatic functions in ASL. These include, but are not limited to, functioning as a pronoun or a determiner (see Valli and Lucas 2000). The use of indexing to the source has not been studied from a grammatical perspective in interpreted discourse. Nevertheless, interpreters have been found to use indexing to the source to provide attribution regarding the content of an utterance being relayed. Like eye gaze, index-to-source can provide information about a shift from one speaker to another as well as the location of the source, but not information about the identity of the source. It can also assist the interpreter in clarifying the meaning of a relayed pronoun. For example, the interpreter might point to the appropriate primary participant while simultaneously signing a first-person pronoun to clarify that the pronoun does not refer to the interpreter (Metzger 1995a, 1999).

Name or Description

Stating the name of the source is a very explicit way of providing source attribution. Short of naming the source, the interpreter can provide a description of the source, using hair length, hair color, or attire as a means of indicating who is responsible for the utterance being relayed. Identifying a speaker before reporting the speaker's utterance is a form of constructed dialogue introducer (Ferrara and Bell 1995). For example, in ASL discourse signers may sign the name or role of a character or person from their narrative followed by that character or person's utterance. (Metzger 1995b, Liddell and Metzger 1998). This practice is another example of interpreters' using strategies found in the narrative discourse of native signers who are reporting on previous or imagined conversations. But interpreters use them to report on current (or very recent) discourse of primary participants who are present at the interpreted event. Naming speakers or describing them by their appearance provides explicit information about who is responsible for the content of a relaying. It also provides information about a shift in turn to a new speaker. It does not provide information about the location of the speaker.

The four strategies for providing source attribution from English into ASL, body shift, eye gaze, index-to-source, and naming/describing the source, each provide some information relating to the following pieces of information:

1. Location of the source
2. Identity of the source
3. Change in speaker

Several sources (Fleetwood and Metzger 1990; Metzger 1995a, 1999) point out that these three pieces of information are inherent in noninterpreted interactive discourse. That is, in spoken English conversations among hearing native users of English, participants know these three pieces of information simply by virtue of being present in the interaction. This is also true for visual conversational interaction. In ASL conversations among sighted, Deaf, native signers of ASL, all the participants know the location of the source, the identity of the source, and changes in speaker turns simply by virtue of being a part of the conversation. For this reason, Fleetwood and Metzger (1990) and Metzger (1995a, 1999) suggest that in order to achieve interactional equivalence, interpreters would need to provide all three pieces of information throughout an interpreted interaction. Although none of the four strategies identified above provides all this information, interpreters can and do combine them.

Combining Strategies

Several of these strategies can be combined simultaneously to provide the observer with information that is more complete and that includes information about a change in speaker, the identity of the new source, and the new source's general location in the interaction (Metzger, Fleetwood, and Collins 2004). The most explicit possible combination includes naming or describing the speaker while indexing the source and also while using eye gaze and body shift. A second explicit strategy is to name or describe the speaker and index the source, which also identifies a shift in turn, the identity of the source, and the source's location (Metzger, Fleetwood, and Collins 2004).

SOURCE ATTRIBUTION IN ENGLISH

Attribution of source is relevant to all primary participants. In fact, in Deaf-hearing interpreted encounters, one might speculate that hearing participants require more source attribution than Deaf participants do because hearing participants are often first-time consumers of interpreting services. Evidence for this is provided in a conversation between a hearing pediatrician and a deaf mother (Metzger 1995a, 1999). When the interpreter uses first person in translating the mother's information about the baby, the doctor gets confused about who is taking care of the baby, the interpreter or the mother. He not only asks for clarification; he specifically indicates it is the first-person pronoun that caused his confusion.

Although source attribution from ASL into English is of equal or greater importance in ASL-English interpretation, the studies of source attribution cited here have found no occurrences of source attribution in English (Metzger 1995a, 1999; Metzger, Fleetwood, and Collins 2004). Nevertheless, interpreting students can use the following strategies, which can suffice until empirical description improves the list.

1. Using introducers such as "he said" or "she said"
2. Naming speakers, as in "Mrs. Smith is asking . . ."
3. Using descriptions, especially in larger groups, such as "The man in blue . . ."
4. Providing vocal variation to distinguish between signers
5. Gesturing to the source (with limbs or eye gaze)
6. Combining some of the above

This list is more prescriptive than descriptive. What signed language interpreters actually do to attribute source is an excellent area for future research. In the meantime, spoken-language interpreting researchers may be able to offer some suggestions (see, for example, Angelleli 2001, 2003; Wadensjö 1992, 1998).

TEACHING SOURCE ATTRIBUTION

Teaching interpretation students strategies for incorporating source attribution into their interpreting helps students prepare for providing interactional equivalence when interpreting one-on-one or small-group interaction. The following steps are recommended.

1. Review source attribution
2. Observe source attribution

3. Have students practice attributing source
4. Ask students to analyze source attributions in their own interpretations
5. Have students redo as needed, with a focus on these features
6. Try a variety of roleplays, including small-group interaction (see Metzger 2000)

These steps should provide students with the information they need to understand source attribution as well as why it is an important aspect of interaction and why it is requisite for providing interactional equivalence. They should also provide students with models of what source attribution looks like and the opportunity to practice it in developmental steps, first with the controllable video source and then with actual roleplays. It is advisable that students eventually have the opportunity to practice in low-risk, real-world interpreting situations.

In order to accomplish step 1, in which students review source attribution, teachers should have a discussion with them in which the relevance and features of source attribution are identified. Teachers can also provide them with some readings on the topic and offer supportive learning activities such as a worksheet or essay question in which they must describe the relevance of source attribution, the reasons interpreters attribute source, and the ways they do it when interpreting into each of their languages. One good reading related to source attribution (Metzger, Fleetwood, and Collins 2004) compares the features of source attribution in both visual and tactile ASL and in more than one discourse genre.

To assist students in developing an awareness of this feature, teachers can have them observe source attribution by other interpreters (step 2 above). This step could include any or all of the following types of observations:

1. Source attribution modeling during class
2. Video models of source attribution
3. Observations outside the classroom of interpreters who are adept in providing source attribution in their work

Observations of source attribution will likely require teacher input while students begin to develop the ability to see the various and potentially overlapping techniques for attributing source. Ideally, initial observations will be of a source interpretation for which students have a transcription. Transcriptions would allow students to identify source attribution from a videotaped source and also on the paper transcript. This initial step will assist students in recognizing source attribution subsequently and also in analyzing their own use of source attribution in their practice interpretation work. One excellent videotaped source for this activity is Patrie's videotapes from the Effective Interpretation Series published by DawnSignPress: *Interpreting in Legal Settings*, *Interpreting in Insurance Settings*, and *Interpreting in Medical Settings*.

Once students have developed the ability to recognize source attribution, and once they have demonstrated an understanding of how and why it occurs, it is time for them to try to incorporate it into their own work (step 3). Videotapes provide a useful starting point for students, in part because they are not as chaotic as real-world interaction. The relatively controlled switch between turns, as defined by the camera angle, allows students the opportunity to incorporate various features of source attribution in their interpretation with a little less stress than might arise in roleplays with live participants. Students should be asked to analyze their work (step 4). They should identify what forms of source attribution they use and why, and if appropriate they can redo a warm videotape to include different forms of source attribution (step 5). In this manner they have the opportunity to become experienced with more than one form of source attribution. In addition, students can observe in what ways source attribution is different when working with a videotaped source. For example, in many student practice videotapes with one deaf and one hearing consumer, there is little interruption or overlap. Asking students to consider this aspect of their practice causes them to think about source attribution in new ways and therefore to develop a deeper understanding of it.

Videotapes are a good starting point for students developing the ability to include source attribution in their interpretations.

However, videotapes do not compare with real-world interaction. For this reason, students should also engage in roleplays with Deaf and hearing participants (step 6). See Metzger (2000) for an in-depth discussion of how to create roleplays most likely to replicate realistic interaction. These roleplays need not be limited to one-on-one interaction. They can also be set up as small-group interactions in order to replicate the turn-taking needed in a meeting or classroom. These roleplays should incorporate actual Deaf and hearing professionals as much as possible (Metzger 2000), with topics that are familiar and appropriate to the individuals who participate. Also, these roleplays should include a post-interpretation discussion in which the interpreting process and the incorporation of source attribution are addressed.

Finally, teachers can offer students a test of what they have learned regarding source attribution. Such an exam could be a paper exam, or it could include analysis of videotaped source material. It might focus only on source attribution, or it might address several features of interpreted interaction that the students are required to study. At the very least, students should be asked to consider how source attribution might be similar or different depending on factors such as setting and number of participants. Better still, students can complete the unit by engaging in further observations of how source attribution varies according to these and other factors.

The steps outlined here are general steps that should be applicable to almost any existing course that focuses on interpreting interaction. They also are applicable to any of the other features identified earlier in this chapter. Ways these steps would apply to other features are discussed in the next section.

Application to Teaching Other Features

The previous section offers a template for teaching not only source attribution but any of the features discussed earlier in this chapter: introductions, attention-getting strategies such as summonses, turn-taking and overlap, responses to questions directed to the interpreter, requests for clarification, and relaying of pronominal reference. To prepare to teach each feature, the teacher would gather information about it from sources referred to in this chapter and elsewhere. Then the teacher could apply the information and potentially relevant video source material to the generic outline below:

1. Review the feature
   a. Identify it
   b. Describe it
   c. Discuss its relevance
   d. Provide readings
2. Present opportunities for students to observe the feature
   a. Model it
   b. Present video models
   c. Have students observe interpreters outside the classroom
3. Have students practice incorporating the feature
   a. Using video source
   b. Using roleplays
4. Have students analyze the feature in their own interpretations
5. Have students redo steps as needed, with a focus on the features
6. Have students try it in a variety of roleplays, including small-group interaction (see Metzger 2000)

Suggestions for arranging roleplays, including pedagogical tools such as a sample roleplay schedule sheet and a sample self-analysis form, are available elsewhere (Metzger 2000).

Following these steps is one way to bring students' attention to features of interpreted interaction that make it unique. By discussing, reading about, identifying, and practicing interpreters' strategies for providing interactional equivalence, students should be better prepared for the work world upon graduation.

CONCLUSION

Interpreters' work is discourse. But interpreting interactive discourse requires more than just relaying the utterances people produce. Interpreters may need to introduce themselves to primary participants and might also briefly explain what it means to participate in an interpreted interaction. This explanation requires finesse because interpreters must make decisions about which language to use at what time and how much to explain. Their decisions relate to their own power and role in the interaction and to those of others, which have tremendous implications when one of the interlocutors comes from a minority community (see Metzger 1995a, 1999).

As seen above, interpreters negotiate numerous aspects of discourse as primary participants ask questions of them, make requests, try to take turns or to gain the attention of other primary participants in ways incompatible with the language or mode used by the other, and so forth. Cokely (2003) finds that in at least in one region of the United States, new graduates of interpreter preparation programs work primarily in one-on-one and small-group interactions. In order to better prepare students of interpretation to face the real world of work they will encounter upon graduation, it is imperative that interpreter educators provide the curriculum and materials students need to gain the skills to negotiate those aspects of discourse that are implicit within or in addition to the relaying of what people say.

References

Angelleli, C. 2001. Deconstructing the invisible interpreter: A critical study of the interpersonal role of the interpreter in a cross-cultural/linguistic communicative event. Ph.D. diss., Stanford University, Stanford, Calif.

———. 2003. The visible co-participant: Interpreter's role in doctor/patient encounters. In *From topic boundaries to omission: New research in interpretation*, ed. M. Metzger, S. Collins, V. Dively, and R. Shaw. Washington, D.C.: Gallaudet University Press.

Baer, A. M. 1991. Tactility in the Deaf community. Paper presented at the Gallaudet University Department of Sign Communication Lecture Series. Washington, D.C.

Baker, C. 1977. Regulators and turn-taking in American Sign Language. In *On the other hand: New perspectives on American Sign Language*, ed. L. Friedman, 215–36. New York: Academic Press.

Chen, C. 1993. Attention getting strategies used by a Deaf adult with Deaf children. In *Gallaudet University communication forum*, vol. 2, ed. E. Winston, 11–19. Washington, D.C.: Gallaudet University School of Communication Student Forum.

Cokely, D. 1992. *Interpretation: A sociolinguistic model.* Sign Language Dissertation Series. Burtonsville, Md.: Linstok Press.

———. 2003. Curriculum revision in the twenty-first century: North-eastern's experience. Project TIEM Online Roundtable Discussion. (Also see chapter 1 in this volume.)

Colonomos, B. 1995. How do we construct meaning (the message)? Unpublished ms. Greenbelt, Md.: The Bilingual Mediation Center.

Ferrara, K., and B. Bell. 1995. Sociolinguistic variation and discourse function of constructed dialogue introducers: The case of *be + like*. *American Speech* 70:265–90.

FitzPatrick, T. 1993. Attention getting strategies used by a Deaf adult with deaf children. In *Gallaudet University communication forum, vol. 2*, ed. E. Winston, 37–50. Washington, D.C.: Gallaudet University School of Communication Student Forum.

Fleetwood, E., and M. Metzger. 1990. *Cued Speech transliteration: Theory and application.* Silver Spring, Md.: Calliope Press.

Gile, D. 1995. *Basic concepts and models for interpreter and translator training.* Amsterdam: John Benjamins.

Gish, S. 1987. "I understood all the words, but I missed the point": A goal-to-detail/detail-to-goal strategy for text analysis. In *New dimensions in interpreter education: Curriculum and instruction*, ed. M. McIntire. N.p.: Conference of Interpreter Trainers.

Liddell, S. K., and M. Metzger. 1998. Gesture in sign language discourse. *Journal of Pragmatics* 30 (6): 657–97.

Mather, S. 1990. Home and classroom communication. In *Educational and developmental aspects of deafness*, ed. D. Moores and K. Meadow-Orleans, 232–54. Washington, D.C.: Gallaudet University Press.

———. 1994. Adult-Deaf toddler discourse. In *Post-Milan-ASL and English literacy: Issues, trends, and research*, ed. B. D. Snider, 283–97. Washington, D.C.: Gallaudet University College for Continuing Education.

Metzger, M. 1995a. The paradox of neutrality: A comparison of inter-preters' goals with the realities of interactive discourse. Ph.D. diss., Georgetown University, Washington, D.C.

———. 1995b. Constructed dialogue and constructed action in American Sign Language. In *Sociolinguistics in Deaf Communities*, ed. C. Lucas, 255-71. Washington, D.C.: Gallaudet University Press.

————. 1999. *Sign language interpreting: Deconstructing the myth of neutrality*. Washington, D.C.: Gallaudet University Press.

————. 2000. Interactive role-plays as a teaching strategy. In *Innovative practices for teaching sign language interpreters*, ed. C. Roy. Washington, D.C.: Gallaudet University Press.

Metzger, M., E. Fleetwood, and S. Collins. 2004. Discourse genre and linguistic mode: Interpreter influences in visual and tactile interpreted interaction. *Sign Language Studies* 4 (2):118–37.

Roy, C. 1989a. A sociolinguistic analysis of the interpreter's role in the turn exchanges of an interpreted event. Ph.D. diss., Georgetown University, Washington, D.C.

————. 1989b. Features of discourse in an American Sign Language lecture. In *The sociolinguistics of the Deaf community*, ed. C. Lucas, 231–51. San Diego: Academic Press.

————. 2000a. *Interpreting as a discourse process*. New York: Oxford University Press.

————, ed. 2000b. *Innovative practices for teaching sign language interpreters*. Washington, D.C.: Gallaudet University Press.

Sacks, H., E. Schegloff, and G. Jefferson. 1974. A simplest systematics for the organization of turntaking in conversation. *Language* 50:696–735.

Sanheim, L. 2003. Turn exchange in an interpreted medical encounter. In *From topic boundaries to omission: New research in interpretation*, ed. M. Metzger, S. Collins, V. Dively, and R. Shaw. Washington, D.C.: Gallaudet University Press.

Schegloff, E. 1972. Sequencing in conversational openings. In *Directions in sociolinguistics*, ed. J. Gumperz and D. Hymes, 346–80. New York: Holt, Rinehart, and Winston.

Schegloff, E., and H. Sacks. 1973. Opening up closings. *Semiotica* 7: 289–327.

Seleskovitch, D. 1998. *Interpreting for international conferences*. 3rd ed. Washington, D.C.: RID.

Simmel, G. 1950. Quantitative aspects of the group. In *The sociology of Georg Simmel*. Glencoe, Ill.: Free Press.

Tannen, D. 1984. *Conversational style: Analyzing talk among friends*. Norwood, N.J.: Ablex.

Valli, C., and C. Lucas. 2000. *Linguistics of American Sign Language: An introduction*. 3rd ed. Washington, D.C.: Gallaudet University Press.

Wadensjö, C. 1992. Interpreting as interaction: On dialogue interpreting in immigration hearings and medical encounters. Linköping Studies in Arts and Sciences. Stockholm, Sweden: Linköping University.

————. 1998. *Interpreting as interaction*. London: Longman.

Winston, E. A. 1991. Spatial referencing and cohesion in an American
    Sign Language text. *Sign Language Studies* 73:397–410.
———. 1992. Space and involvement in an American Sign Language lec-
    ture. In *Expanding horizons: Proceedings of the 12th national Convention of
    the Registry of Interpreters for the Deaf*, ed. J. Plant-Moeller, 93–105.
    Silver Spring, Md.: RID Publications.

JEMINA NAPIER

Teaching Interpreting Students to Identify Omission Potential

IN MY STUDY of interpreters of Australian Sign Language (Auslan) to English, I found that interpreters' production of omissions was influenced by their familiarity with the context of the situation and the content of the message they were interpreting, which was a university lecture (Napier 2002). They made a range of omissions; some were strategic, some were based on a reason, and some were errors. I determined that an omission had occurred "when information transmitted in the source language with one or more lexical items does not appear in the target language, and therefore potentially alters the meaning" (Napier 2002, 121). I found that the interpreters involved in the study had high levels of awareness in respect to the omissions they made and why they made them. This type of awareness is called metalinguistic awareness and can be defined as "the ability to focus attention on language and reflect upon its nature, structure and functions" (Garton and Pratt 1998, 149). It also includes the abilities to select and process specific linguistic information and to consider what aspects of language are relevant in any particular context. It can be argued, therefore, that interpreters ought to develop this type of awareness so that they can make the most appropriate linguistic choices and decisions in order to render the best possible interpretation within a particular context.

To benefit interpreter educators, I used my research findings to develop an analysis tool for teaching interpreting students to identify the "omission potential" of an interpreting assignment or an

123

interpreted message and the factors that may influence the types of interpreting omissions they produce and why. This chapter introduces an omission taxonomy and step-by-step process of analysis that can be used with students to identify patterns of omissions and the factors that might influence their choice of what to omit and when. By tapping into students' metalinguistic awareness, interpreter educators can actually encourage students to reflect on the reasons omissions were made and the impact of the omissions on interpreted messages.

ANALYSIS TECHNIQUES

The most effective analyses of interpretations give consideration to message equivalence and to the interactive influences on an interpretation. This philosophy is heavily reflected in the contributions to a recent work (Roy 2000b) on training sign language interpreters (Winston and Monikowski 2000; Pollitt 2000; Metzger 2000; and Davis 2000).

It is typical, however, for analysis to concentrate on the identification of errors or miscues in the form of additions, omissions, substitutions, and intrusions (e.g., Cokely 1992). I felt it important to acknowledge the positive and negative effects of producing omissions within an interpretation in that an interpretation can be considered successful even if omissions are made; but at the same time, it is important to recognize that omissions can be produced in error.

INTERPRETING OMISSIONS

As I have mentioned, studies of interpreting have typically regarded omissions as errors. But an analysis of an interpreted message cannot just count the number of errors; it must also measure the success of communication. In this way, interpreters can identify both the strengths and the weaknesses of their interpretations.

Scholars such as Livingston, Singer, and Abramson (1994) and Wadensjö (1998) have recognized that interpreters may, on the basis of their understanding of meaning and cultural relevance, make a conscious decision to produce an omission and that making certain omissions does not necessarily have a negative impact on the overall message conveyed in the interpretation. For example, explicit visual information conveyed in American Sign Language (ASL) or Auslan may be omitted from a translation because if conveyed in spoken English, it would sound peculiar (Padden, 2000/1).

The omission taxonomy below specifically recognizes that lexical omissions are produced by interpreters strategically or on purpose, as well as in error.

Omission Taxonomy

1. *Conscious strategic omissions* occur when interpreters make conscious decisions to omit meaningful information because omitting it will make the message more effective. Interpreters use their linguistic and cultural knowledge to decide which information from the source language makes sense in the target language, which information is culturally relevant, and which may be redundant.

2. *Conscious intentional omissions* occur when interpreters make an omission that leads to a loss of meaningful information. Interpreters are conscious of these omissions and make them intentionally because they don't understand the particular linguistic unit (word or phrase) or could not think of an appropriate equivalent in the target language.

3. *Conscious unintentional omissions* also lead to a loss of meaningful information. Interpreters are conscious of the omission but make it unintentionally because they hear the linguistic unit and decide to "file it" and wait for more contextual information or depth of meaning before interpreting it. Because of further source language input and lag time, however, interpreters forget the particular linguistic unit and omit it.

4. *Conscious receptive omissions* lead to a loss of meaningful information and occur when interpreters cannot properly hear and decipher what the linguistic units are because of poor sound quality.

5. *Unconscious omissions* lead to a loss of meaningful information because interpreters are unconscious of the omission and do not remember hearing the omitted linguistic units.

Omission Taxonomy as an Analysis Tool

In applying theory to practice and honing analysis skills, interpreters, interpreting students, and interpreter educators can use the omission taxonomy to become more aware of the linguistic choices and decisions to be made when making omissions, leading to a better understanding of the factors that may influence their interpretations in various contexts.

Practical Application in the Classroom

Step 1: Interpreting Task

This analysis tool works best with interpretation of a monologue. Monologues can be defined as a piece of text in which one participant in the interactive discourse has the floor, selects the subject matter, which may focus on a theme or related themes, and decides when the text starts and finishes (Cokely 1992). I would suggest, therefore, that teachers search for a source text of no more than five to seven minutes in length, such as an extract from a university lecture or conference presentation. This exercise can work in both language directions, so teachers should include a range of spoken and signed texts and have available either a written transcript or a written translation of each text.

After selecting a text, the student should be given maximal opportunity to watch or listen to the text and read the transcript. In so doing, the student can research any unfamiliar vocabulary and prepare a discourse map (see Winston and Monikowski 2000) of the text and its ideal interpretation. In beginning the interpreting task, teachers should caution that students cannot ask for repeats and should continue interpreting through the text. This process allows for the identification of both positive and negative omissions, in a

Table 1. Example of Noted Omissions

Line number	Text
1	In 1991, three authors, <u>Judy</u> Reilly, <u>Marina</u> McIntire, and <u>Ursula</u>
2	Bellugi, published a study called "Babyface." Now Bellugi is well
3	known in the area of sign language research, but she is equally well
4	known for her work on early language acquisition across the board. And
5	"Babyface" the study that these three authors, er, published, was called,
6	<u>was subtitled</u>: "a new perspective on universals in language
7	acquisition." And really why they were looking at sign language
8	acquisition was from the perspective of <u>what it tells us, or told us, about, erm</u>, what it told us about the nature of language acquisition in a range of languages.

Note: Underlined words represent omissions by the student.

context in which the interpreter cannot ask for clarification or repetition, which often happens in the real world. In this way, the teacher and student can identify how and why the omissions are produced as "coping strategies" for dealing with the message and any linguistic problems (Napier 2002).

The student is then videotaped interpreting the text. The teacher observes the interpretation from just outside the peripheral vision of the interpreter so as not to present a distraction. While observing, the teacher underlines parts of the transcribed text that are omitted. See table 1 for examples of noted omissions. As teachers listen or watch the interpretation, they will be looking up and down at the transcript when they are noting omissions, so they may miss some aspects of the interpretation. The aim of the exercise is to identify patterns of omission production, however, so it is not necessary to identify every single omission. Typical patterns of omission production, identified in my original study (Napier 2001), are discussed later in this chapter.

Although the interpretation is also being videotaped, I have found that underlining the text is the most expedient way of identi-

fying omissions. Identifying them provides a means for the interpreting student and the teacher to examine the identified omissions,
as well as look for others, when reviewing the videotape.

Step 2: Task Review

The task review should happen almost immediately after completion of the interpreting task, while the interpretation is fresh and
students remember their thoughts. In this step the teacher and the
student watch the videotape and pause the tape every time an omission is noted (either by the teacher on the transcript or by the student). Students should reflect on whether they were aware of the
omission and, if aware, on the reasons for the omission. If working
with an interpreting student with little or no interpreting experience, the teacher should lead the review, point out omissions, and
ask students to recall and comment on what they were thinking at
the time. Teachers will probably find that less experienced students
will not initially have the confidence or competence to clearly identify omissions themselves and will rely on the teacher to guide
them. However, the teacher can encourage the students to be as reflective as possible because reflection is part of the experiential
learning process.

Once guided, the students will likely be amazed at how much
they can recall of their thoughts at the time and the reasoning behind the omissions. Notes of the student's comments should be
made on the transcript of the source text next to the relevant noted
omissions. Notes should focus on the key reasons identified by the
student for each omission. Keeping in mind the omission taxonomy,
the teacher can focus on comments that reveal whether the omission was strategic, intentional, unintentional, receptive, or unconscious. An example of reflective commentary notes can be seen in
table 2.

The examples in this chapter are taken from very experienced interpreters who participated in the original study. Teachers ought to
be mindful that newer students might not be as articulate with their
comments. For example, instead of "redundant information," newer

Table 2. Examples of Reflective Commentary Notes

Text	Commentary
	First names not necessary—almost
In 1991, three authors, <u>Judy</u> Reilly, <u>Marina</u> McIntire, and <u>Ursula</u> Bellugi, published a study called "Babyface." Now Bellugi is well known in the area of sign language research, but she is equally well known for her work on early language acquisition across the board. And "Babyface" the study that these three authors, er, published, was called, <u>was</u> <u>subtitled</u>: "a new perspective on universals in language acquisition." And really why they were looking at sign language acquisition was from the perspective of <u>what it tells us, or told us, about, erm</u>, what it told us about the nature of language acquisition in a range of languages.	redundant information—the key is to get the surnames. Remember thinking would be waste of time if fingerspelled first names, as would take up valuable time, when could concentrate on something else.

Don't even remember hearing that bit—no recollection of it at all.

Unnecessary repetition—detracting from the meaning. |

Note: Underlined words represent omissions by the student.

students may say something like "they don't need to know that information," or instead of "unnecessary repetition," they may say "he said it again and I don't think it needed to be included again." This review can be an opportunity for the teacher to introduce students to the appropriate vocabulary for discussing and analyzing interpretations.

Step 3: Categorization of Omissions and Discussion

On completion of the review, the teacher and interpreter go through the omissions and categorize them according to the omission taxonomy outlined in this chapter. Table 3, drawn from my original study of interpreting omissions by Auslan-to-English interpreters (Napier

Table 3. Examples of Omission Categorization

Subject comments	Omission category
For me, this [sign] "not enough" . . . was enough to cover both . . . [words 'inadequate' and 'incomplete']. I felt like I would've been signing the same thing twice, and looking for a different way to sign it when it means the same thing.	Conscious strategic (CS)
I couldn't think of how to translate "resilience," I just couldn't, I just couldn't. I had trouble with that, I just couldn't think of a way to do that.	Conscious intentional (CI)
I forgot that. I meant to put that in and it just . . . by then he was on to the next sentence.	Conscious unintentional (CU)
I couldn't hear him; his voice went down.	Conscious receptive (CR)
I didn't hear that at all!	Unconscious (U)

2001), shows a few participants' comments about selected omissions and the corresponding omission type identified.

Once the teacher and students have categorized the omissions, they can discuss what patterns appear in what categories. One way to do that is to count the number of omissions in each category and consider factors that may have influenced the production of omissions, such as register of language, familiarity with the topic, use of technical terminology, and others. Table 4 shows the pattern of omissions produced by two of the participants in the original study of interpreting omissions (Napier 2001). The source text used in the original study was an excerpt from a university lecture about deaf children's acquisition of sign language.

By identifying possible influencing factors, interpreters can apply their metalinguistic awareness in determining why they made particular omissions while interpreting a particular piece of text. They can use this awareness in predicting factors that may influence their

Table 4. Examples of Patterns of Omission Production

Interpreter	Number of each omission type					
	CS	CI	CU	CR	U	Total
2	7	15	5	11	12	50
8	9	2	5	3	10	29

Note: CS: conscious strategic, CI: conscious intentional, CU: conscious unintentional, CR: conscious receptive, and U: unconscious.

omission production in future interpreting situations, that is, the *omission potential* of any interpreted message. Inevitably some of the omissions will be unconscious, and the interpreter will have no control over them. The rest, however, will be made deliberately, and this exercise raises interpreters' awareness of their areas of strength and weakness and may also give them a tool for determining whether to accept an interpreting assignment.

Consider, for example, the factors that influenced the interpreters featured in table 4. Interpreter 2 did not have a university education and was not familiar with the topic. As a consequence, she made a number of erroneous omissions as she struggled with the content and delivery of the source text. Interpreter 8, however, had a university education, was familiar with the lecture topic, and was thus more comfortable with the terminology used, the density of the text, and the pace of delivery. Table 5 shows some of the same two interpreters' comments concerning their feelings about their interpretations.

Interpreter 2 may be able to predict that if offered a university assignment or something to do with language acquisition, the assignment's omission potential would be rather high; in other words, she would likely make more detrimental than productive omissions. She could thus make an informed decision whether to accept the assignment. This example helps beginners understand the tasks they might face. Interpreter 8, on the other hand, could predict that her potential for detrimental omission production in this context would

Table 5. Interpreters' Comments

Interpreter	Comments
2	I was hindered by my lack of higher education. . . . I haven't studied since I was fifteen. I found this task hard because of the academic language used in universities. I didn't have enough knowledge of the subject matter, the English language, or the terminology used.
8	I have a university education . . . so I am familiar with the language use and with university situations, so I wasn't intimidated by that, but the ideal is to have knowledge of the content. I was comfortable with the level of language because I have interpreted this type of lecture lots of times before. . . . Plus my educational background helped me to deal with the level of language—I'm used to the university environment and the language use.

be minimal and could therefore accept this type of work with confidence. In taking this approach to identifying omission potential, both interpreters could evaluate ways to be better prepared to interpret university-level lectures, such as reading beforehand, talking to the instructor, researching topics on the Internet, and similar steps.

Step 4: Prediction for Second Interpreting Task

Step 4 involves the teacher's selecting a new source text that presents the interpreter with a similar interpreting task. The student should be given preparation time, with at least one opportunity to watch, listen to, or read the source text, as appropriate. The teacher then asks the student to identify the omission potential of the upcoming interpretation based on the preparation and reminds the student to consider the factors that may influence the interpretation. For example, a university lecture titled "What Is Deaf Culture?" may lead interpreter 2, who is not familiar with academic language but is extremely comfortable with the topic of Deaf culture, to predict she would feel confident of making fewer erroneous omissions in this instance.

Step 5: Second Interpreting Task, Review and Discussion

The teacher and interpreter then follow the same process as outlined in steps 1, 2, and 3, filming the second interpreting task, performing a task review, and categorizing and discussing the omissions.

Step 6: Comparison of Omission Patterns

In this step, teacher and student compare and discuss the omission patterns identified in the first and second interpreting tasks and consider what factors influenced each interpretation and the types of omissions produced. For example, if a high rate of conscious intentional omissions were identified in a text on a topic the student was unfamiliar with, the omission pattern may be attributed to the lack of understanding of the topic and its technical vocabulary. Alternatively, a pattern of conscious strategic omissions may emerge when a student is familiar with a text topic and its terminology. The whole process can be repeated several times, using texts that incorporate features of language use found in various contexts, such as a radio announcement, a joke, a television advertisement, a narrative, a set of directions, and more.

Alternatives

Once students get used to this analysis technique, the teacher can gradually reduce the amount of preparation, first eliminating the opportunity for additional research, for example, then withholding the transcript, then not permitting students to watch or listen to the text, and ending with minimal preparation. In this instance, the teacher would provide the student with only the topic and an explanation of the context. After a somewhat successful beginning with optimum levels of preparation and after identifying patterns of omission production with good preparation, the students can begin to hone their skills by identifying patterns of omission production with minimal preparation. By this stage, they will be able to distinguish between their linguistic coping strategy strengths and weaknesses under ideal and potentially stressful working conditions. This process allows students to recognize sources of demand and how they may assert control (Dean and Pollard 2001) through the use of omissions.

If using this analysis technique in a professional development workshop, trainers might find that working interpreters are more adept at reflecting on the reasons for their omission production than are newer interpreting students. If this is the case, the teacher presents working interpreters with the transcript on which the teacher has underlined omissions and asks them to self-analyze what they omitted and why. The interpreters can make notes on the transcript and then discuss and analyze their transcriptions in small groups, categorize the omissions according to the omission taxonomy, and evaluate factors that may have influenced their omission production. This technique works well as a peer-review process as well as a teacher-student process.

AIM OF THE EXERCISE

The process of analysis and identification of omissions gets interpreters thinking about their processing, what they have problems with and why, and also their level of consciousness during an interpretation. Students develop skills in analysis and self-reflection and become familiar with equivalence-based interpreting. As it is a labor-intensive method, once familiar with the technique, students can work in pairs or small groups to analyze each other.

This process also allows interpreters to understand that "an interpretation can never convey 100 percent of the information imparted in a message, as there will always be a level of information loss, of which even the interpreter is unaware" (Napier 2002, 162), but heightened awareness of unconscious omissions may also lead interpreters to develop more confidence about what information they do retain and the equivalence and effectiveness of the overall message. In the original study, I found that of a total of 341 omissions produced by ten interpreters, 27 percent were unconscious and 26 percent were conscious strategic omissions (Napier 2001). This statistic demonstrates that unconscious omissions and strategic (i.e., productive) omissions are almost equally common and that all omission types need to be considered when analyzing interpretations: omissions produced deliberately and constructively and omissions produced in error. This process of omission identification is important in raising interpreting students' awareness of the role of omissions in interpretations. In a survey of sixteen spoken and sixteen sign language interpreters in Austria, Pöchhacker (2000) found that 44 percent of spoken language interpreters approved of omitting utterances, compared with only 7 percent of sign language interpreters. This is a perception that needs to be changed.

CONCLUSION

For the purpose of analyzing interpretations, interpreter educators ought to recognize that interpreting is a discourse process (Roy 2000a) and that interpreters and students need to give consideration to the context in which they are interpreting and the factors that might influence their interpretation choices. Interpretation does not take place in a vacuum; it is a living, evolving, and changing entity, much the same as language. Two interpreters will often provide completely different interpreted renditions of the same piece of text according to various factors that influence their linguistic choices. Nida (1998) identifies four factors that interpreters need to consider: (1) the appropriate language register to be used in the context; (2) the expectations of the target audience members as to the type of translation they expect to receive; (3) distinctive sociolinguistic features of the source text (e.g., language register, use of technical language, familiarity with content); and (4) the medium employed for the translated text (i.e., written, spoken, or signed). In giving consideration to these factors, interpreters and students can analyze their production of interpreting omissions within a context of omission types and thus improve their metalinguistic awareness of the interpreting process. By improving their awareness, they will

be in a better position to predict the omission potential of interpreting assignments and make informed decisions about accepting
those assignments.

Acknowledgments

Thanks to those interpreters who participated in the original research project (Napier 2001) that led to the identification of different omission types and the resulting omission taxonomy. I can't
mention you by name here, but you know who you are. Thanks also
to those people who have supported me in the writing of this chapter, through either discussing the content or proofreading.

References

Cokely, D. 1992. *Interpretation: A sociolinguistic model.* Burtonsville, Md.:
    Linstok Press.
Davis, J. 2000. Translation techniques in interpreter education. In
    Innovative practices for teaching sign language interpreters, ed. C. Roy, 109–
    31. Washington, D.C.: Gallaudet University Press.
Dean, R., and R. Q. Pollard. 2001. The application of demand-control
    theory to sign language interpreting: Implications for stress and inter-
    preter training. *Journal of Deaf Studies and Deaf Education* 6 (1):1–14.
Garton, A., and C. Pratt. 1998. *Learning to be literate: The development of
    spoken and written language.* Oxford: Blackwell.
Livingston, S., B. Singer, and T. Abramson. 1994. Effectiveness compared:
    ASL interpretation versus transliteration. *Sign Language Studies* 82:
    1–54.
Metzger, M. 2000. Interactive role-plays as a teaching strategy. In
    Innovative practices for teaching sign language interpreters. ed. C. Roy, 83–
    108. Washington, D.C.: Gallaudet University Press.
Napier, J. 2001. Linguistic coping strategies of sign language interpreters.
    Unpublished Ph.D. diss., Macquarie University, Sydney, NSW,
    Australia.
———. 2002. *Sign language interpreting: Linguistic coping strategies.*
    Coleford, UK: Douglas McLean.
Nida, E. 1998. Translators' creativity versus sociolinguistic constraints. In
    Translators' strategies and creativity, ed. A. Beylard-Ozeroff, J. Králová,
    and B. Moser-Mercer, 127–36. Philadelphia: John Benjamins.

Padden, C. 2000/1. Simultaneous interpreting across modalities. *Interpreting*, 5 (2):169–86.

Pöchhacker, F. 2000.The community interpreter's task: Self-perception and provider views. In *The critical link 2: Interpreters in the community*, ed. R. P. Roberts, S. E. Carr, D. Abraham, and A. Dufour, 49–66. Philadelphia: John Benjamins.

Pollitt, K. 2000. Critical linguistic and cultural awareness: Essential tools in the interpreter's kit bag. In *Innovative practices for teaching sign language interpreters*, ed. C. Roy, 67–82. Washington, D.C.: Gallaudet University Press.

Roy, C. 2000a. *Interpreting as a discourse process*. Oxford: Oxford University Press.

———. 2000b. *Innovative practices for teaching sign language interpreters*. Washington, D.C.: Gallaudet University Press.

Wadensjö, C. 1998. *Interpreting as interaction*. London: Longman.

Winston, E. A., and C. Monikowski. 2000. Discourse mapping: Developing textual coherence skills in interpreters. In *Innovative practices for teaching sign language interpreters*, ed. C. Roy, 15–66. Washington, D.C.: Gallaudet University Press.

ROBERT G. LEE

From Theory to Practice: Making the Interpreting Process Come Alive in the Classroom

ONE OF THE greatest challenges in teaching interpreting is providing students with both an abstract knowledge of a theory of interpretation and a personal understanding of the application of the theory. The ability to recite the stages in a specific theory is not a particularly helpful skill for a student interpreter. Along with knowing the outline of a model, students must be able to experience the stages, thereby developing an awareness of their own control of the interpreting process. A primary goal of teaching the interpreting process is providing students with a feeling of control, something they can take away from the classroom and exercise on their own. The following exercise is designed to help students in both acquiring knowledge of the interpreting process and understanding their control of it. I begin by outlining the underlying model framing the exercise, then provide some preliminary notes, and finally explain the exercise itself.

BACKGROUND

Having taught interpreting in both workshop and university settings, I have been struck that many interpreters, novice or experienced, talk about the application of a theory of interpretation but rarely put theory into practice outside a learning environment. In

138

working with student interpreters, I want to instill an understanding of the interpreting process from the very beginning to help them integrate the process in their work in and out of the classroom.

THEORETICAL FRAMEWORK

The model I am working under is Dennis Cokely's *sociolinguistic model of the interpreting process* (Cokely 1992). I have chosen this model for a variety of reasons. First, I feel that the level of detail it offers is helpful in clarifying for students the discrete stages that interpreters proceed through in order to successfully interpret between two languages. Second, the model clearly delineates those specific skills needed at various points in the interpreting process. The ability to know and articulate one's work in terms of subparts can be very helpful in looking at successful and less successful interpretations. Third, Cokely's taxonomy of miscues is very helpful in having students discuss why a specific interpreted message is successful or not.[1]

Some have claimed that Cokely's model is too complicated for students to learn, let alone work with in a classroom setting. I disagree; I think we underestimate the ability of students to both learn a complex theory of interpreting and apply it. I have found that students may be somewhat daunted by the model initially but that clear presentation and examples of application help students to learn the model as outlined by Cokely as well as use it in discussing their own work and the work of their classmates. In addition, students have reported that the ability to look at the stages of their work and see successes in some stages is quite helpful. Often students perceive their own work in a binary fashion: as either all good or (more often, unfortunately) all bad. Having the ability to look for

---

1. Cokely defines a miscue as "a lack of equivalence between the s(ource)L(anguage) message and its interpretation or, more specifically, a lack of concordance between the information in an interpretation and the information in the s(source)L(anguage) message it is supposed to convey" (Cokely 1992, 74).

Table 1. Stages of the Cokely Model

Cokely's stage	Short description	Reminder
Message reception	The act of physically receiving the source message through the appropriate channel	Perceive
Preliminary processing	The act of recognizing the source message as a linguistic signal	Recognize
Short-term message retention	The act of storing enough of the source signal to achieve an understanding of the message	Chunk
Semantic intent realized	The act of understanding the source message (Importantly, as Cokely states, "Ideally, of course, the semantic intent of the message realized by the interpreter is that originally intended by the speaker") (Cokely 1992, 127)	Understand
Semantic equivalent determined	The act of finding equivalents in the target language for the concepts expressed in the source message	Analyze
Syntactic message formulation	The act of (mentally) fashioning an equivalent target message	Formulate
Message production	The act of articulating the target message	Produce

success (or lack thereof) in stages of the process is empowering to students; they can see where they are using strategies that are successful and where they need to improve.

Table 1 provides a brief outline of the Cokely model. The reader is referred to Cokely (1992) for a more complete discussion. I have provided a description of each stage in terms of acts in order to underscore to students that interpreters are actively engaged in the work at all stages of the process. In addition, I have added a one-word reminder that captures the essential focus of each stage.

Discussion of the model is sometimes helpful in having the students grasp what the model is capturing. I begin with the idea that every day, almost automatically, students receive messages from other people, decode them, and understand them. In addition, students every day have ideas, encode them, and express them. There-

Message Reception	*Semantic Intent Realized*
Preliminary Processing	Semantic Equivalent Determined
Short-term Memory Retention	Syntactic Message Formulation
Semantic Intent Realized	Message Production
Stages dealing with Source Language	**Stages dealing with Target Language**

Figure 1. Process stages by language focus

fore, individual components of the interpreting process are already a part of the skill set that the student brings to the classroom (of course, students vary in their ability to deal with the languages they work with). Students begin to realize that when perceiving and understanding a message, they are going through the first four stages of the model (*message reception* through *semantic intent realized*). When expressing their own ideas, they go through the last four stages of the model (*semantic intent realized* through *message production*). *Semantic intent realized* is the stage when one understands what someone has said and also formulates what to say to another.

Another way to frame subparts of the model is to look at which language (source or target) is the primary focus at each stage of the process. This shift in focus is outlined in figure 1.

Note that semantic intent realized appears in both listings. This is the "overlap" stage, in which the source message is understood by the interpreter and in which the interpreter begins to cast the message in the target language. This stage can be considered both the *output* of the source language stages and the *input* to the target language stages. Figure 2, discussed more below, pictures it as the interface between the source and the target languages rather than as both of them.

One area that is not overtly addressed in the model is monitoring, which is the part of the task in which the interpreter makes sure the process is going smoothly, checking for and repairing errors in both content and form as well as analyzing and incorporating feedback from the audience or a team interpreter. Monitoring is a metaskill; it requires a high level of knowledge of one's own work and the ability to analyze what is happening in the moment. I feel it is important that students realize, as early as possible in their training, that monitoring is a vital part of the interpreting process. In order to make the idea of monitoring more concrete, I use analogies to a factory, with the interpreting process being akin to an assembly line. I present students with the idea that an interpreter may do three types of monitoring:

1. Process monitoring: This type of monitoring is an "overall" monitor. It is the process by which an interpreter assesses the big picture, looking at the incoming source language and seeing if the overall process is going well. I compare this type of monitor to the supervisor of a factory looking down from overhead to see that all is flowing smoothly through the assembly line.

2. Preproduction monitoring: This type occurs between the *syntactic message formulation* and *message production* stages. In it an interpreter "tries on" the target interpretation before actually articulating it (I believe this is similar to what Betty Colonomos means by "rehearsal" [Colonomos 1989]). The analogy here is the final inspector, the person who inserts the "Inspected by Number 7" tag we often find in new articles of clothing.

3. Postproduction monitoring: Interpreters sometimes catch themselves after uttering something that is a mismatch between the source and target messages (or some other type of miscue)—something that prompts a repair in the interpretation.[2] This type of monitoring can be compared to a factory worker looking out the door, seeing a substandard product being shipped, and issuing a recall.

---

2. Note that in this form of monitoring, it is the interpreter who recognizes the miscue. The fact that an end consumer of interpreting may catch a miscue is a similar issue but external to the interpreter's cognitive processes.

When interpreters are overwhelmed by aspects of the process (be it source message speed, density of information, or internal filters), monitoring is often the first element of the process to stop working. We have known for many years that the number of interpreting errors or miscues increases as an interpreter becomes fatigued, but recent research has shown that interpreters' recognition of errors becomes impaired as well. A recent article promoting the use of interpreters in teams cited a study of conference interpreters as follows:

> During the first 30 minutes the frequency of errors—as measured with an elaborate error scale—rose steadily. The interpreters, however, "appeared to be unaware of this decline in quality," according to the report, as most of them continued on task for another 30 minutes. (Vidal 1997, citing Moser-Mercer, Kunzli, and Korac)

Because the activity of interpreting, as well as the concept of monitoring, can be overwhelming, I have designed an exercise that separates the tasks while providing students with experiences of the interpreting process. In the exercise described below, some of the work of monitoring, usually done *internally* by an interpreter, is performed *externally* by a peer.

Figure 2 is a visual representation of the stages of the interpretation process grouped into source and target language tasks. It includes the one-word "reminders" of the focus of each stage as well as the location of pre- and postproduction monitors.

Preliminaries to the Exercise

Before introducing the model to the students, I discuss with them some background assumptions:

- We all have only a limited amount of cognitive energy for all the tasks we have to do (I often refer to this amount as a "bank" of energy). These tasks include, but are not limited to, getting the message, processing the message, remembering the message, self-talk, worrying, monitoring the process, monitoring the audience, predicting, repairing, looking for feeds from a team member,

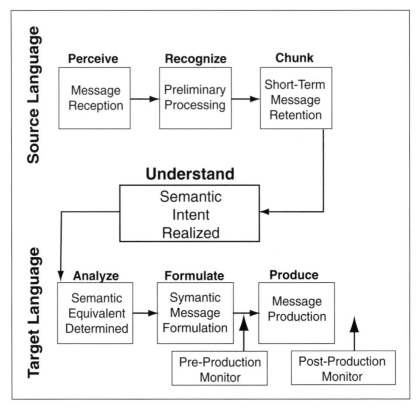

Figure 2. Modified Cokely model

deciding whether or not to take a feed, processing feedback from the audience, processing feedback from the team, and more.

• The more energy used at the beginning of the process, the less available later in the process.

• Conversely, using less energy at the beginning leaves more energy for later stages of the process.

• Using energy wisely is one of the most important skills an interpreter can have. Another term for it is *resource allocation*. (It has also been called *process management*, but it involves more than just the interpreting process, including, for example, self-talk.)

- Being aware of where they are in the process allows interpreters to control the process, not be controlled by it.
- Discussing the decisions that led to an interpretation is more helpful than discussing whether a particular interpretation is right or wrong.

To get students into the habit of looking at interpreting through the lens of this model, I ask them to draw the model on the board for every class meeting. Any student can do it; I just ask that it be on the board before class begins. Students can use notes to write the stages or do it from memory; they can also do it as a team. By drawing the model on a regular basis, students become used to the vocabulary of the stages. In addition, having the model above the area where the students will be working serves as a reminder that we are discussing the interpreting work, not the interpreter.

The Exercise

The objective of this exercise is for students to gain experience with the various stages in the interpreting process as well as with the concept of monitoring the interpretation. One student is responsible for providing an interpretation of a text, and two other students divide up the interpreting task based on the model described, one focusing on those stages dealing with the source language, the other focusing on those stages that deal with the target language.[3] I have called this the "three-chair" exercise because it involves the three students working together, seated in front of a television, as shown in Figure 3.[4]

---

3. An additional benefit to this exercise was pointed out to me by Cindy Roy. It allows students to get used to the idea of team interpreting as well as how and when they may need to receive feeds. A component that can be added is having students look at the types of information they ask for and the types of information they give when working in a team.

4. I have done this exercise primarily with ASL as the source language and English as the target language because this direction is logistically easier and because students often feel they "don't know where to begin" when interpreting from ASL to English. With minor modifications, the exercise could be done with English as the source language.

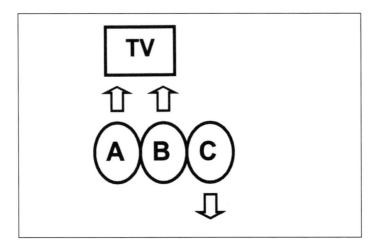

Figure 3. Student placement for interpretation process exercise. Arrows indicate the direction the students face during the exercise.

The source text that is on the television can be one that is familiar to the students, or it can be a novel text.[5] A fifteen-to-twenty-minute text is the right length for this exercise because it contains enough information for students to work with and provides them familiarity with the speaker and subject as the text goes on. The student in the middle, student B, is the one ultimately responsible for producing an interpretation of the text. Students taking a turn in the B position are given the remote control for the VCR and can stop (but not rewind) the tape when they feel they have enough information to provide an interpretation for the text up to that point. Student B can do this without any help but may get assistance from the other two students. Student A, who is also watching the text, can provide assistance with the source-language part of the task (i.e., the first three stages of Cokely's model). That is, student A can repeat what was said, paraphrase it, or in another way provide the

---

5. There are benefits and drawbacks to using either a novel or a familiar text. One advantage of a novel text is that students can get a feel for applying the process as one would in real life. An advantage of using a known text is that students may have more time and energy to focus on the individual stages of the process. One approach is to start students with a known and predictable text and work up to using the exercise with completely novel texts.

information that student B needs, but only in the source language.[6] All communication between students A and B is to be in the source language. Student C, who is not watching the source text, can provide assistance only in the target language (i.e., the last three stages of Cokely's model). Student B can ask C specific questions about target-language production (but not interpretation of meaning), such as "What is the word for the person who runs an entire school system?" or "Does [example] sound like grammatical English?" In this way, student C can function as the preproduction monitor, assisting in the formulation of the target message.

After student B provides the interpretation of the relevant portion of the text, student C can provide immediate feedback about the target-language production (but not the accuracy of the message vis-à-vis the source). Some examples:

- The interpretation is somehow not clear. For example, the interpretation contains a pronoun with an unclear or ambiguous antecedent. (Student B: "So John took it with him." Student C: "What does 'it' refer to?")
- The interpretation contains a word that seems not to make sense in the context of the utterance. (Student B, talking about building a house: "So he hit the nail with a haddock." Student C: "A haddock?")
- The interpretation is unintelligible or inaudible.

When student B is satisfied with the interpretation of a portion of the text, he or she restarts the tape and continues, stopping when ready to interpret another portion of the text. Looking at a part of the text, getting whatever assistance is needed, and producing an interpretation of that portion counts as one whole turn. It is usually best to allow a student at least five turns (depending on the length of each portion of text).

---

6. Note that, should student A be unable to provide assistance, the instructor can serve as a backup, providing information in the source language that student B asks about. Indeed, one may start the exercise this way, with the instructor modeling the types of information the source-language assistant can give.

When first using this exercise with a class, I have found it helpful to have the students stop and talk about the experience, beginning with student B. This can be done after the first round of five or so turns, long enough to give the students a chance to get used to the exercise. It is important to guide students to talk about the work in a specific way: focusing on the process, talking about stages, and looking at decisions made. For example, a student who needs to have a portion of the source text repeated may say "I definitely got through *message reception* and *preliminary processing*; I am not sure if I had an issue with *short-term memory retention* or *semantic intent realized*" as opposed to saying "I missed it." Further discussion may help the student uncover what was problematic. The teacher can pose such questions as the following: Did you understand all the signs you saw but not realize what the speaker's point was? Were there any unfamiliar signs? Did you just not perceive some part of the message and therefore could not come to an understanding of it? Helping students evaluate what they just did provides them with tools to analyze their own work more thoroughly by themselves.[7]

After student B is finished, students A and C can talk about how they felt the process went. Finally, the rest of the students in the class should be noting how the process goes. Students should think about the following questions:

- What seemed to drive the interpreter's decisions to stop the text?
- How did the interpreter take advantage of the other two students in the process?
- Which stages in the process seemed fairly easy for the interpreter? Which presented more challenge? What is the evidence on which you base your observations?

---

7. It is entirely possible for student B to complete this task without ever turning to A or C for help. In this case, the teacher can ask student B to reflect on the interpretation and the experience of going though the stages as an internal process. Because part of the goal is for students to experience portions of the task, it is important that student B be able to articulate the decisions made, not merely produce an interpretation. In addition, the teacher can ask students A and C about their experience of focusing on only one portion of the entire process.

After the discussion has run its course, the students should rotate roles: student A (who was watching the source text) becomes the interpreter, student B becomes student C, and student C moves to the role of student A. The process continues, allowing each student at least five turns and a break for discussion. After all three students have been in all three roles, a wrap-up discussion is helpful. The teacher can lead students to discuss the following questions:

- In which role did you feel most comfortable? Least comfortable? Why do you think that was so?
- At what point(s) did you need to turn to one of the other students for assistance? What drove your decision to get help? Did you receive the kind of help you needed? Why or why not?
- What was it like being in either of the "less active" roles (i.e., A or C)?

I have found that this exercise can also be diagnostic. Those students who struggle with the source language (due to either skill limitations or psychological factors) tend to turn to the source-language "helper" (student A) more often. Those who struggle with the target language (or who are less confident in this area) tend to turn to student C more often. Instructors can note both the type and the quantity of help that students elicit from the source- and target-language assistants. In addition, a student's self-report of comfort levels when in each role can be helpful in identifying patterns of strength and weakness as well as areas where students feel more confident or less confident about their skills.

Conclusion

The exercise presented here is an attempt to provide students with concrete experiences with the stages of an abstract model of the interpreting process (the Cokely model). In addition, introducing the concept of monitoring the interpreting process as a *part* of the process is key to helping students be in control of their own work. By laying a foundation of theoretical understanding, outlining basic assumptions about the purpose of models, and allowing students to perceive the various subparts of the interpreting task, we can bring students to a deeper understanding of their own work as interpreters.

ACKNOWLEDGMENTS

I wish to acknowledge those who have been a part of the development of my thinking along these lines. The exercise itself was partly developed while I was teaching in the American Sign Language-English Interpreting Program at Northeastern University in Boston, Massachusetts. I am grateful to the students in the program as well as to Dennis Cokely, chair of the program, for helping me refine this exercise. An earlier version of the diagram showing the separate steps in the process (figure 2) was partly developed while working with the Project TIEM Master Mentor Program in Boulder, Colorado, in the summer of 2002. I would like to thank Betsy Winston and Christine Monikowski as well as the Cohort One students for their feedback on the framing of the model in this way. Any errors or mistakes are solely my own.

REFERENCES

Cokely, D. R. 1992. *Interpretation: A sociolinguistic model.* Burtonsville, Md.: Linstok Press.

Colonomos, B. M. 1989. The interpreting process: A working model. Unpublished manuscript.

Moser-Mercer, B., A. Kunzli, and M. Korac. Prolonged turns in interpreting: Effects on quality, physiological and psychological stress (pilot study). *Interpreting* 3(1):47–64.

Vidal, M. 1997. New study on fatigue confirms need for working in teams. *Proteus: Newsletter of the National Association of Judiciary Interpreters and Translators* 1 (winter):1. Available from http://www.najit.org/proteus/back_issues/vida12.htm.

MIEKE VAN HERREWEGHE

Teaching Turn-Taking and Turn-Yielding in Meetings with Deaf and Hearing Participants

IF DEAF PEOPLE and nonsigners attend a joint meeting, they need at least one sign language interpreter to accomplish successful communication between them.[1] It is generally assumed (especially by "outsiders," i.e., nonsigners who have no experience in communicating with Deaf signers) that in such "mixed" meetings the presence of a sign language interpreter guarantees equal participation of both parties, Deaf people and nonsigners. Other researchers and I have shown that if a chairperson does not act to or does not know how to guarantee equal participation, perhaps because he or she is not well acquainted with Deaf culture, it falls to interpreters to step out of their neutral, usually passive role as conduit and resolve the problem (Van Herreweghe 2002; Roy 1989, 1993; Metzger 1999).

Interpreter students need training to manage the intercultural process of turn-taking and turn-yielding in mixed meetings without actually interfering in this delicate communicative system. One way this training can be achieved is by means of roleplays and simulations. According to Metzger (2000, 85), interactive roleplays have

---

1. It is customary to write "Deaf" with a capital letter D when referring to deaf people regarding themselves as members of a linguistic and cultural minority group of sign language users regardless of their degree of hearing loss, and "deaf" with a small letter d when not referring to this linguistic and cultural minority group.

151

three primary objectives. Students need to be able to do the following:

1. Recognize and identify features of interactive discourse
2. Understand interpreters' strategies for coping with interactive discourse
3. Apply strategies for coping with interactive discourse.

This chapter discusses these objectives in relation to multiparty meetings. The next section focuses on features of interactive discourse, more specifically turn-taking mechanisms, in spoken-language and sign language meetings, and the differences between the two are explored. The third section deals with interpreters' strategies in interpreted multiparty meetings, and the fourth looks at roleplays and simulations as teaching tools through which interpreter students can internalize these strategies.

Turn-Taking Mechanisms in Multiparty Meetings

Turn-Taking Mechanisms in Spoken-Language Conversations

Conversation analysts Sacks, Schegloff, and Jefferson wrote a seminal paper (1974) on the structure of turns in conversation. They noted that any current speaker can select the next speaker by producing a turn that includes language to give over the turn and perhaps identifies the next speaker. This selecting of the next speaker is typically the first part of a pair, and the second part is subsequently produced by the next speaker. However, a first-pair part alone does not always give the turn over to the next speaker. Another study (Lerner 1993, 224) identified other ways in which the next speaker can be selected. For example, a speaker can look at the next speaker while turning over the turn, look at and simultaneously name the next speaker, look at someone and use the pronoun "you," with the gaze indicating who "you" is, or just say "you" without looking if it is clear to whom "you" refers. All of the "rules" above can come into play when conversations are exhibiting one-at-a-time speakers. However, turn-taking is more complicated than that.

Edelsky (1981) distinguishes between two models of turn-taking in everyday interactions. She claims that on the one hand there is a single or singly developed floor, similar to the model presented by Sacks, Schegloff, and Jefferson (1974), and on the other hand there is a collaborative, or collaboratively developed, floor, which is potentially open to all participants at the same time. Edelsky came to this conclusion when she analyzed five university subcommittee meetings of people who were not only colleagues but also close friends. She noticed that the conversations alternated between both types of floor. The singly developed floor was mostly used in talk that was more firmly oriented toward business (i.e., in more formal settings), whereas the collaborative floor was mostly used in talk that strayed from the agenda and had the more interpersonal goal of maintaining social relations (and which was as such also more informal). Moreover, Coates (1994, 1997a, 1997b) claims that women having informal conversations with female friends tend to adopt a collaborative floor, whereas men in informal conversations with male friends tend to adopt a single floor and prefer a mode of turn-taking typically used in formal meetings.

In formal meetings with a chairperson, turn-taking may follow a system in which the chairperson allocates the turns. Larrue and Trognon (1993) describe this "system of third party designation of next speaker" as follows:

> Firstly, when the current speaker indicates the end of his turn, the chairman is the one who intervenes by calling upon the next speaker. Secondly, the order of the speakers is dictated by the requests to speak expressed as the meeting progresses. Someone who wishes to speak raises his hand. The chairman writes the requester's name on the list. He will grant that speaker a turn when all preceding individuals on the list have spoken. (181)

Meetings in which the chairperson has tight rein on the interaction are, at best, an ideal. As we all know, many meetings don't always attain this ideal because sometimes a speaker takes over the floor without formally asking the chair to get it, there is overlap between speakers, or a collaborative floor develops when the chair-person lapses in controlling the turns.

Turn-Taking Mechanisms in Signed Conversations

Turn-taking mechanisms in signed conversations have not been studied all that frequently (see Mather 1987; Martinez 1995). Baker (1977) found that in conversations between two signers, there was no need to focus on the selection of the next speaker or the alloca-tion of the next turn. However, she was able to discern the follow-ing turn-claiming regulators by the addressee during the speaker turn:

a. Optional increase in size and quantity of head-nodding, often accompanied by an increase in size and quantity of indexing the speaker
b. Optional switch to palm$_a$ [i.e., palm up with heel raised higher than fingertips]
c. Movement out of rest position to get speaker's attention; may in-clude indexing, touching, or waving hand in front of speaker
d. Switching to –GAZE when speaker is +GAZE (may include postural shift, looking up (as if thinking while preparing to sign), facial signaling of forthcoming question, disagreement, etc.)
e. Initiating turn (interrupting) and repeating first few signs until speaker is +GAZE and has yielded the floor or until speaker suppresses addressee's turn-claim. (219)

In the course of my research (Van Herreweghe 2002), I looked at turn-taking mechanisms in an all-sign, chaired (and thus formal) meeting and concluded that the ways in which a speaker can self-select were similar to the signals described by Baker. However, I also found additional ways in which Deaf speakers get the floor. For example, one Deaf speaker stretched out a 5-hand with the palm away from the speaker and the fingers up, just above the table. This was used only once and in the context of relinquishing the floor to another speaker but also wanting the floor back.

Another variant, again not used very often, ran as follows: A signaled to B, the person sitting next to the current speaker, to warn the current speaker that A wanted the next turn. This was not used very often, probably because it is a fairly cumbersome method involving a third party. It was used only when A thought that the current speaker had not noticed that A wanted the next turn, and thus it was used only when waving a hand, tapping the table, or something similar did not prove successful.

One striking feature of this meeting was that self-selection was never pure self-selection because the current speaker retained the power to allocate the next turn by means of eye gaze. Whenever more than one person wanted to take a turn, and however they signaled, such as by waving a hand, the current speaker would select the next speaker by means of gaze direction. The person at whom the current speaker was looking was (usually) allocated the next turn.

This is quite different from what was found by Coates and Sutton-Spence (2001) in their analysis of friendly, informal conversations within small groups of Deaf friends. They claim that because Deaf studies have until now focused mostly on formal talk (especially on classroom talk), researchers have assumed that signed conversation is typically a singly developed floor. However, from Coates and Sutton-Spence's informal conversational data, it is obvious that a collaborative floor is quite possible. What's more, this was clearly the preferred option of female signers in that study, whereas men friends shifted from one mode to another.

> Just like hearing friends, Deaf friends, especially women friends, exploit the potential of the collaborative floor to construct talk jointly. They accept the risk of (occasionally) making contributions which are not seen by others because this risk is outweighed by the capacity of polyphonic talk to symbolize solidarity and connection. This is clearly salient in talk among friends. Further research will establish whether or not the collaborative floor is drawn on by Deaf interactants in other, more formal contexts. (Coates and Sutton-Spence 2001, 527)

In my data from a formal, chaired meeting of seven Deaf members of the board of directors of the Flemish Deaf Association, this was clearly not the case, but further research in this area is needed.[2]

Differences between Spoken Conversations and Signed Conversations

When turn-taking mechanisms in a spoken conversation are compared to those in a signed conversation, a number of differences stand out:

• According to Lerner (1993), in spoken-language conversations one of the most important ways of giving over the turn was using someone's name. In the all-sign meeting, however, names or other identifying terms were never used when speaking to another person and turning over the turn. They were used when talking about someone, but never as an addressing device. This difference should not be ignored by interpreters; it means that when they are interpreting from a spoken language to a sign language, it is important to use names rather than something like "the person sitting there" (which would be a literal translation of a pointing sign). Conversely, when they are interpreting in the other direction, there is no need to fingerspell the names of the participants or use name signs because pointing signs, for instance, would be the preferred translation.

• In my data from an all-sign meeting, eye gaze proved to be an extremely important and powerful regulator by which the current speaker selects the next speaker.

• In line with the previous point, there seems to be a considerable difference in turn-taking between chaired spoken-language meetings and chaired signed meetings. Whereas in the former the chairperson controls the allocation of the next turn, in the latter the current speaker typically gives over the next turn to another

---

2. For more information about the Flemish Deaf Community, see Van Herreweghe and Vermeerbergen 1998.

by means of eye gaze. This is a very important difference. It means that in chaired meetings with Deaf and non-Deaf participants, Deaf participants have to give up this system of turn-taking because when their eye gaze is directed at the interpreter, they cannot select the next speaker. Obviously, interpreters need to be aware of this difference.

THE ROLE OF INTERPRETERS IN CHAIRED MULTIPARTY MEETINGS

Up till now I have discussed only data from (multiparty) conversations in which one language is involved. Although it is important for interpreters to be aware of how turn-taking occurs in one-language group meetings, they must also be aware of the differences when two languages are involved.

> When an interpreter interprets between a spoken language and a sign language, such as English and ASL, participants can easily misgauge or misunderstand when it is appropriate to attempt to take a turn in the conversation because the linguistic signals are not even based in the same mode. Thus, an interpreter is likely to encounter professional situations in which both participants attempt to take a turn at the same time, and the interpreter must be prepared to handle that situation appropriately (see Roy 1989, 1993). (Metzger 2000, 86)

In the past, interpreters were viewed "as passive, neutral participants whose job it is to mechanically transmit the content of the source message in the form of the target language" (Roy 1993, 342). However, interpreters have an active role "in managing the intercultural event of interpreting" (Roy 1993, 341). This became obvious when Roy examined, among other things, simultaneous talk or overlap in a dyadic conversation (one nonsigner, one Deaf signer) with an interpreter. She concluded that interpreters have four options in the case of overlap:

> The interpreter can stop one or both speakers and, in that way, halt the turn of one speaker, allowing the other speaker to continue. If the interpreter stops both speakers, it is possible that one of the

primary speakers will decide who talks next, or the interpreter may make that decision.

The interpreter can momentarily ignore one speaker's overlapping talk, hold (in memory) the segment of talk from that speaker, continue interpreting the other speaker, and then produce the 'held' talk immediately following the end of the other speaker's turn. . . .

The interpreter can ignore the overlapping talk completely.

The interpreter can momentarily ignore the overlapping talk, and upon finishing the interpretation of one speaker, offer a turn to the other primary speaker, or indicate in some way that a turn was attempted. (Roy 1993, 350)

In all these cases, the interpreter ultimately resolved turn problems created by overlap and thus became an active participant. Roy's analysis involved turn-taking in only a dyadic conversation. It is interesting to see that the strategies used by interpreters in such a situation also occur in chaired multiparty meetings.

Requesting a Turn and Turn Allocation

In a meeting with Deaf signers and nonsigning participants and one or two interpreters, the nonsigning participants can fairly easily signal to the chair that they would like to get the floor.[3] They can seek eye contact with the chair by means of a small hand movement, or if the chair is not looking at them, they can make a subdued noise such as a cough or a "hm," or clear the throat or something similar.

For Deaf participants there is quite a difference between meetings with one sign language interpreter and meetings with two. If, in a meeting with two sign language interpreters, Deaf participants want to request a next turn, they can signal to the chair, in which case they have to lose eye contact with the interpreter and seek eye contact with the chairperson. Alternatively, they can maintain eye contact with the interpreter and signal that they would like the next

---

3. Because I looked only at meetings with a hearing chair (Van Herreweghe 2002), I can discuss turn-taking phenomena and so forth only in the context of meetings with a hearing chairperson. It would be very interesting to see whether their turn-taking is similar to turn-taking in meetings with a Deaf chairperson, but to my knowledge no such research has been carried out.

turn, expecting one of the interpreters to signal the chair. Although this seems the best strategy, requesting a turn can nevertheless be quite complicated for a Deaf participant:

> In example 2, R. seems confused by the fact that he got the floor from the chairperson while the voice-to-sign interpreter was still signing. Thus, he does all the checking. After he is convinced that the current speaker has stopped talking and after having checked with the chairperson, he signals to the sign-to-voice interpreter by raising his hand that he is going to start. All of this checking, of course, takes time, so a fairly long pause occurs between the hearing speaker's last utterance and R.'s first. (Van Herreweghe 2002, 86)

Ideally the chairperson in this situation would wait for the interpretation to be finished before allocating the next turn. However, a chairperson who has no experience with this kind of interaction may find these protocols difficult to bear in mind, and in that case the interpreter may have to intervene and ask the chair to wait until the interpretation is finished before allocating the next turn.[4]

The whole process of signaling and getting a turn is even more difficult when there is only one interpreter. In my research, overlap occurred quite frequently in such meetings, especially when the interpreter was still interpreting and a Deaf participant requested the next turn or started a turn. It happened often that the chairperson did not notice the request or the beginning of a turn (sometimes because the chairperson was the person holding the floor). In such cases of overlap, the interpreter adopted various strategies (very similar to Roy's strategies [1993]):

- Sometimes the interpreter decided to halt the turn of the chairperson and allowed the Deaf participant to start a turn. This frequently occurred when the chairperson's turn was at a transition moment that was recognized as such by the interpreter and so seemed an appropriate moment to stop the turn. At this point the

---

4. Even if the chairperson is acquainted with this kind of interaction, it is sometimes difficult to take account of the interpretational lag because it automatically slows down the pace of the meeting, and that is not always looked upon favorably in a world where "time is money."

interpreter often decided who would get the next turn and thus managed the direction and flow of turn-taking.

- Most of the time the interpreter did not interpret the signer's utterances. This most commonly occurred when the chairperson either forgot to allocate turns (which sometimes happened in the meetings analyzed), so that (hearing) people self-selected, or when the chair allocated the next turn before the interpreter had finished interpreting. Because of the interpretational lag, this often meant that the Deaf participants were too late to request the next turn.

- The interpreter at times attempted to remember one speaker's talk and produce it later, but then failed to do so. In one meeting, different people talked at the same time. The interpreter interpreted one person while, presumably, trying to hold in memory the overlapping talk of another participant, intending to interpret it consecutively. She soon realized that there was too much overlapping talk to hold in memory, signed to the Deaf participants that she couldn't interpret because different people were talking at the same time, and stopped signing. In this strategy the interpreter chose not to resolve the problem caused by overlap but simply stopped interpreting and allowed other participants to resolve the problem. When the interpreter, who automatically attracts a lot of people's visual attention, suddenly stopped signing, her strategy had an instant impact on all the participants.

Self-Selection and Source

It was mentioned above that formal meetings do not always follow a singly developed floor pattern but sometimes use a collaborative floor. In chaired meetings, this obviously is not an ideal situation, but it is a realistic one. In cases of a collaborative floor, there is overlap and participants self-select. Methods and situations vary.

- Self-selection of a signer when a hearing person is speaking seems to be extremely difficult. In my research, self-selection hardly ever occurred in this situation and, if it did, it was problematic. In the meeting with only one interpreter, it resulted in loss or overlap, as I discussed above. In a meeting with two interpreters, the interpreting lag made it difficult for the interpreter to know when to interrupt a speaker when a signer, who is also caught by the lag of interpreting, had self-selected. Thus, there is a need for interpreters to be explicitly aware of discourse structure. Elements of language in both a spoken language and a sign language often mark a transition-relevant moment at which interpreters can interrupt a nonsigning speaker when a signer has self-selected.

- Successful self-selection of a signer can occur only when the eye gaze of the person already signing is directed at the person wishing to self-select and not at the interpreter. In the interpreted meetings I studied, there were some such instances, but fairly often the signers realized that it was necessary to check with the chairperson before taking the floor. The chairperson had to take into account the time lapse between what was being signed and the interpretation and had to ask the signer to wait until the sign-to-voice interpreter had finished. Again, these procedures may be difficult for a chair who is not acquainted with interpreted meetings.

- Self-selection of a nonsigning participant occurred more frequently, possibly because the chairpersons were also nonsigners. Self-selection of a hearing participant has to be indicated by the interpreter. Whenever a participant initiates a turn in a spoken language, it is important that the interpreter interpret not only the content of that utterance but also the source of the turn because the source is an inherent part of the utterance.[5] In a multiparty meeting it is very important to remember source attribution because the eye gaze of the Deaf participants is directed at the interpreter, and if the interpreter does not indicate who initiated a

---

5. In this respect I differ from Metzger (1999, 101), who calls this an "interpreter-generated utterance." To me, source attribution is not "interpreter-generated" but an inherent part of the utterance that also needs to be interpreted.

turn, Deaf participants can become confused. In my research I encountered the following example:

> The chairperson allocates the next turn to one of the hearing parents by saying her name. The interpreter, however, does not indicate that the chairperson had said something (i.e., the name of the next speaker), but immediately points at the hearing parent, thus giving the Deaf participants the impression that the hearing parent had self-selected. (Van Herreweghe 2000, 94)

Moreover, the interpreter quite frequently forgot to indicate a turn change, as in the following example:

> Here, the interpreter interprets what the chairperson says (but not the short back-channeling utterances by the hearing parent) and follows with the interpretation of the hearing parent without a pause or an indication of the fact that a different person is speaking. Presumably, the Deaf participants thought that the chairperson was still talking, although after a while, they noticed that the chairperson was not saying anything anymore, and they quickly glanced at where the hearing parents were sitting, probably to find out who was talking. This glancing around occurred, however, after the hearing parent had already talked for some time. When the interpreter did not attribute the source of the utterance, the Deaf participants obviously lost information. (Van Herreweghe 2002, 94–5)

Written Texts in Multiparty Meetings

A further difference between signed and spoken meetings is related to the way in which written material is treated.[6] In spoken-language meetings it is generally the custom to distribute papers and immediately start discussing them (although sometimes participants are given time to read), meaning that participants listen to the explanations and look at the papers at the same time.

---

6. I would like to stress that the following discussion is based only on the meetings analyzed in my earlier study (Van Herreweghe 2002). Further research will have to show whether similar phenomena occur in other meetings in other countries, in other cultures, etc.

In most sign language meetings, however, papers are distributed and participants are given time to read them; then, to resume the conversation, the signer usually checks whether the other participants have stopped looking at the papers and, if this is not the case, will either tap the table or ask a participant to warn a still-reading neighbor that conversation will start again. While discussing the papers, the signer may show relevant passages to the participants so that everyone knows what part is being discussed. In spoken-language meetings these devices are generally not necessary.

In mixed meetings these different behaviors can clash. A chairperson who is aware of the differences can give all participants enough time to read a text under discussion and then, after making sure everybody knows that conversation is starting again, discuss it while pointing at the relevant passages.[7] However, if the chair is not aware, the interpreter may need to address this cross-cultural difference.

ROLEPLAYS AND SIMULATION GAMES AS LEARNING ACTIVITIES

Metzger (2000) discusses interactive roleplays as a teaching strategy. However, simulations also prove very useful. Simulations have been described as follows:

> A simulation is an activity which is a "classroom copy" or "model" of real-life events. The classroom represents the place where the events take place and the participants are the people involved. Essential background information is given in the form of texts, recordings and documents (such as newspaper articles or radio broadcasts). . . . A simulation isn't just a long roleplay activity, because you will not be playing a role, but also drawing on your own experiences, making decisions and solving problems. In a simulation you will often be

---

7. Although this wasn't studied in my earlier study (Van Herreweghe 2002), I can imagine that something similar holds for overhead projector transparencies or PowerPoint presentations. From personal experience I know that Deaf participants frequently have to look at what is being projected and at the interpreter at the same time.

working as a member of a team, sharing the decision-making and problem-solving with each other. . . . Like real life, a simulation is "open-ended"—there are no "right answers" to the problems you are asked to solve. What happens in a simulation depends on the decisions made and the actions taken by you and your fellow-participants. (Jones 1983, 1)

In my opinion, both roleplays and simulations (or a combination of both) are excellent teaching tools for focusing on interpretational strategies in a multiparty meeting.

As a preparation for such activities, the students first need to build up their metalinguistic awareness of turn-taking phenomena in spoken, signed, and interpreted meetings. This can be accomplished through reading about the differences and looking at videotapes of various types of meetings. Then I would move to roleplays, which, in the beginning, can be short and involve only a limited number of students (and no other participants). In the next step, students participate in more elaborate roleplays, possibly with outside participants, and finally they engage in one or more longer simulations.

In the roleplays and simulations, the students can be the participants in the meetings themselves. Certain kinds of roles can be given to them via role cards. This step may be controversial, even ethically problematic to some people, because some students take on the role of deaf participants. One way to achieve some reality is to give these students ear plugs or head phones. When the students' hearing is blocked, they can experience participating in a meeting in which a chair may not control the meeting tightly and does not take into account the interpretational lag. If the student interpreter assumes a passive, conduit role and also forgets to mark source attribution, for instance, then students get a sense of when it might be appropriate for the interpreter to intervene. It is therefore important that every student take a role of deaf participant during one of the roleplays or simulations.

The roleplays and simulations can cover various types of settings in which various types of participants are involved. Moreover, in each meeting there can be a shift between one interpreter and two interpreters.[8] Furthermore, overhead projector transparencies or PowerPoint presentations should be used, and papers should be distributed halfway through the session. Some suggestions for settings follow.

1. A multiparty meeting in which a chairperson who is well acquainted with this kind of meeting (preferably the teacher) closely controls it. In such a setting it will hardly be necessary for the interpreter to engage in the management of the interaction. This setting represents an ideal situation and is a good one to start with.

2. A multiparty meeting chaired by a nonsigner who does not know anything about Deaf culture but is used to chairing spoken-language meetings and is also familiar with the topic of the meeting. Half of the participants are nonsigners and half take the role of Deaf participants. Students must decide when it is appropriate to intervene so that Deaf participants are able to participate on equal footing.

3. A multiparty meeting with a chair who does not know anything about Deaf culture and with only one Deaf participant. The Deaf participant is familiar with the topic under discussion and is used to participating in mixed interpreted meetings. The other participants are hearing. It will be interesting to see how this meeting differs from the previous setting. This time there is only one Deaf participant, but the Deaf participant knows what it means to be Deaf in a multiparty meeting.

4. A multiparty meeting chaired by a Deaf person and with a mixed audience of hearing and Deaf participants. Although such a meeting has not been described in this chapter, a simulation of this type would be interesting.

It is important that each of these roleplays or simulations be videotaped so that the students' experiences as both participants and interpreters can be discussed in the postroleplay phase. It might be necessary to use two or even four video cameras and possibly split-screen equipment. Planning needs to be taken care of well in

8. Moreover, for the longer simulations, team interpreting could be incorporated, and two to four interpreters could be involved.

advance of the roleplay or simulation session. If one or more of
the participants are not videotaped, the class will not be able to
discuss the whole process of turn-taking and turn-yielding and the
interpreter's role in managing them, which obviously is the ultimate
goal of these sessions.

It is of course important to devise roleplays or simulations that
are relevant for the culture and situation students live and work in.[9]
Here are two examples.

• A rather informal meeting of parents of children who are in the
same kindergarten. Some of the parents have put older children
through kindergarten, but others are new to the situation. The
parents have various occupations (these should be decided on beforehand, preferably reflecting the students' own interests). The
meeting is about the organization of a small party at which all the
parents can get better acquainted with each other. Because some
of the parents are hearing and some are Deaf, one or two sign language interpreters are necessary. One of the parents will act as
chairperson.[10] Make sure that at least one of the "deaf" participants has an important role (perhaps as a restaurant manager who
will cater the party). The participants have to make a number of
decisions: date and place of the party, what they will bring (food,
drink, etc.), who will prepare the food, who will decorate the
room, who will do the cleaning up afterward, who will bring
plates and cups or do the dishes afterward, etc. They also have to
write up an invitation (so that written material is present in the activity as well). Because not all the parents know each other, they
will have to introduce themselves before they can talk about the
party. As this is a rather informal meeting, it is to be expected that
from time to time the floor will develop into a collaborative floor.
If the chair doesn't deal with that, the interpreter(s) will have to.

---

9. For more information about sign language interpretation in Flanders, see Van
Herreweghe and Van Nuffel 2000.

10. If there is not enough time to have more than one role play or simulation focusing on
multiparty communication, it might be a good idea if the teacher takes on the chairperson
role and changes the style of chairing from very tight to very loose.

• (The following example would have to be adapted for the country in which it is used. The description here should provide a fruitful starting point.) A very formal public meeting about a possible adjustment of the students' village and country planning. The meeting is chaired by the municipal counselor in charge of the new plans (who has never met a Deaf person before). The engineer who designed the new plans is also present to answer technical questions. The council would like to execute all of the plans, but a public meeting is mandatory beforehand. Moreover, if there are complaints, the plans will have to be changed. The village and country planning will be explained using old and new maps of the village and the surrounding area. Some of the proposed renovations are a new industrial area on the outskirts of the village, a new road to this industrial area, a new rural area in which no new houses can be built and in which the existing houses can be occupied only by farmers, and changes in the village center. The other participants in the meeting (hearing and one or more who simulate hearing loss or are really Deaf) are inhabitants of the village and have various occupations: a local farmer who lives close to the new industrial area, a carpenter who lives in the village center (but who may want to locate a workshop in the new industrial area because of certain benefits), shopkeepers in the village center, and others, and also people who work somewhere else but live in the village, some of whom live close to where the new road is proposed. Because the chair is not acquainted with interpreted meetings, the interpreters will have to step out of their conduit role from time to time. However, because the meeting is very formal, a singly-developed floor can be expected.

Because sign language interpreters work in so many different types of settings and cultures, teachers must develop their own detailed roleplays or simulations. The outcome of such activities is completely unpredictable because it entirely depends on the contributions of the participants, so such simulations are a challenge for any teacher involved in teaching sign language interpreting. Nevertheless, I strongly believe these activities prove invaluable in teaching students how far they can go in the management of the intercultural process of turn-taking and turn-yielding in chaired meetings with Deaf and hearing participants without actually interfering with the meeting.

REFERENCES

Baker, C. 1977. Regulators and turn-taking in American Sign Language. In *On the other hand: new perspectives on American Sign Language*, ed. L. Friedman, 215–36. New York: Academic Press.

Coates, J. 1994. No gap, lots of overlap: Turn-taking patterns in the talk of women friends. In *Researching language and literacy in social context*, ed. D. Graddol, J. Maybin, and B. Stierer, 177–92. Clevedon: Multilingual Matters.

———. 1997a. One-at-a-time: The organisation of men's talk. In *Language and masculinity*, ed. S. Johnson and U. Meinhof, 107–129. Oxford: Blackwell.

———. 1997b. The construction of a collaborative floor in women's friendly talk. In *Conversation: Cognitive, communicative and social perspectives*, ed. T. Givon, 55–89. Philadelphia: John Benjamins.

Coates, J., and R. Sutton-Spence. 2001. Turn-taking patterns in Deaf conversation. *Journal of Sociolinguistics* 5/4: 507–29.

Edelsky, C. 1981. Who's got the floor? *Language in Society* 10:383–421. Repr. in D. Tannen, *Gender and conversational interaction*, 189–227. Oxford: Oxford University Press, 1993.

Jones, L. 1983. *Eight simulations: For upper-intermediate and more advanced students of English: Participant's book*. Cambridge: Cambridge University Press.

Larrue, J., and A. Trognon. 1993. Organization of turn-taking and mechanisms for turn-taking repair in a chaired meeting. *Journal of Pragmatics* 19 (2):177–96.

Lerner, G. H. 1993. Collectivities in action: Establishing the relevance of conjoined participation in conversation. *Text* 13 (2):213–45.

Martinez, L. B. 1995. Turn-taking and eye gaze in sign conversations between Deaf Filipinos. In *Sociolinguistics in Deaf communities*, ed. C. Lucas, 272–306. Washington, D.C.: Gallaudet University Press.

Mather, S. A. 1987. Eye gaze and communication in a deaf classroom. *Sign Language Studies* 54:11–29.

Metzger, M. 1999. *Sign language interpreting: Deconstructing the myth of neutrality*. Washington, D.C.: Gallaudet University Press.

———. 2000. Interactive Roleplays as a teaching strategy. In *Innovative Practices for Teaching Sign Language Interpreters*, ed. C. Roy, 83–108. Washington, D.C.: Gallaudet University Press.

Roy, C. 1989. A sociolinguistic analysis of the interpreter's role in the turn exchanges of an interpreted event. Ph.D. diss., Georgetown University, Washington, D.C.

———. 1993. A sociolinguistic analysis of the interpreter's role in simultaneous talk in interpreted interaction. *Multilingua* 12 (4):341–63.

Sacks, H., E. A. Schegloff, and G. Jefferson. 1974. A simplest systematics for the organization of turn-taking for conversation. *Language* 50 (4):696–735.

Van Herreweghe, M. 2000. *Language choice and active participation in meetings with Deaf and hearing participants in Flanders.* Paper presented at the international conference *Text and talk at work*, August 2000. Ghent University, Belgium.

———2002. Turn-taking mechanisms and active participation in meetings with Deaf and hearing participants in Flanders. In *Turn-taking, fingerspelling, and contact in signed languages: Sociolinguistics in Deaf communities*, vol. 8, ed. C. Lucas, 73–103. Washington, D.C.: Gallaudet University Press.

Van Herreweghe, M., and M. Van Nuffel. 2000. Sign (language) interpreting in Flanders. *Journal of Interpretation* :101–27.

Van Herreweghe, M., and M. Vermeerbergen. 1998. *Thuishoren in een Wereld van Gebaren.* Gwent: Academia Press.

ANNA-LENA NILSSON

False Friends and Their Influence on Sign Language Interpreting

DURING MANY years of interpreting, I have noticed that sign language interpreters will sometimes use an odd turn of phrase when interpreting into a spoken language. Interpreters utter words and phrases that range from sounding silly to incorrect—thereby running the risk of making the interpretation sound monotonous, non-idiomatic, or downright incompetent. Looking further into this matter, I came to realize that we interpreters say things when interpreting that we would never say when speaking for ourselves. This affects not only the impression we make on those listening to our interpretation but also their impressions of the deaf person whose signed discourse we are interpreting. Looking for the reasons behind this behavior, I discussed the issue with both colleagues in the interpreting field and students of sign language and sign language interpreting. I ended up with a number of possible reasons for the phenomenon, some of which will be presented here, along with a number of ideas for exercises that I have used to make students aware of the pitfalls that will face them when they start interpreting. Awareness, mainly linguistic awareness, turns out to be one of the keys to avoiding the problems discussed here. This chapter is based to a large extent on the concept of false friends (which will be introduced and discussed below) and how it can be used when teaching and analyzing sign language interpreting, especially interpretation from a sign language into a spoken language.

170

This chapter is based on ideas and thoughts that have arisen mainly in my work interpreting between (and teaching) Swedish Sign Language and spoken Swedish. It is my hope, though, that it will be possible for readers to make connections between their respective sign language and the spoken language of their country and to see the resemblance between what I discuss and occurrences in their own language pair, whether it be American Sign Language and American English, British Sign Language and British English, Norwegian Sign Language and Norwegian, and so on, and thus find useful and applicable ideas here.

FALSE FRIENDS

A concept that is of major importance for the rest of this chapter is false friends, or "faux amis." Despite the fact that the concept is frequently used with regard to second-language teaching and learning, as well as in other disciplines, it is difficult to find an established definition of it. In *A Dictionary of Grammatical Terms in Linguistics* (Trask 1993), for example, the concept is not listed at all. The problem with finding a definition has been summed up quite nicely by one scholar as follows:

> False friends can thus, by being directly linked to the concept of linguistic transfer, be regarded as a well-established phenomenon in contrastive linguistics, as well as within language learning and translation. Despite this it can hardly be argued that false friendship is also a well-defined phenomenon. Even though there seems to exist a large amount of intuitive agreement on what is and what is not to be regarded as false friends, the concept is also surrounded by a similarly large portion of fussiness. (Ohlander 1997, 331; my translation)

So we are dealing with a concept that is "well established" without being "well defined." The nearest I have come to a definition is found in *English Synonyms and False Friends*; it reads as follows:

> A large number of English words are astonishingly similar to some Swedish words but have a completely different meaning from the Swedish words. Words like those are usually called *false friends*. (Hargevik and Stevens 1978, 47; my translation)

This definition does not really make the concept "well defined" either; it is based more on a feeling of what is "astonishingly similar" than on hard facts. But it gives us a clear indication of the nature of the phenomenon we are dealing with. The authors also use another definition, based on their knowledge of which English words actually cause problems for Swedish learners, which will be presented below. In general, though, the idea is that false friends are pairs of words from two different languages that sound similar but have different meanings.

WHAT IS SIMILAR?

Swedish is primarily a spoken language, perceived via the auditory channel, but Swedish Sign Language, on the other hand, is perceived via the visual channel. It is therefore difficult to claim that words and signs in the two languages are surprisingly similar (compare Hargevik and Stevens 1978, quoted above). A definition like theirs could actually be used to claim that it is impossible to discuss the issue of false friends in connection with a language pair such as spoken Swedish and Swedish Sign Language (or any other pair of spoken and sign languages). But in doing so, we would lose the opportunity to discuss a number of issues of interest to interpreter trainers, and I will therefore persist in using the concept.

In sign languages, a considerable portion of the linguistic message is expressed by means of nonmanual signals, including movements of the mouth, which carry linguistic meaning, too. Some of the mouth movements used when signing strongly resemble the movements we make with our mouth when pronouncing words of spoken languages. This fact is the reason that it is sometimes claimed that a sign has "Swedish mouth movements," or that the mouth movement that accompanies a sign is "borrowed from spoken Swedish."

> "[S] indicates that the mouth movement is borrowed from Swedish (in reduced or full form)." (*Svenskt teckenspråkslexikon [Swedish Sign Language Dictionary]* 1997, xvi; my translation)

In the following I have decided to regard signs accompanied by such mouth movements as a special case of false friends because it offers me the possibility of anchoring my ideas in an existing frame of thought. As will become increasingly clear, there are also other reasons for considering the links between signs and spoken words and the way they create false friends.

FALSE FRIENDS AND SIGN LANGUAGE TEACHING

One other reason for using the concept false friends in my discussion is that I soon discovered that it was frequently used in sign language programs around Sweden.[1] My discussions with teachers and students of these programs made me realize that a number of signs in Swedish Sign Language were designated false friends. In fact, a limited set of signs (the number and identity of which varied between programs) was taught as "the false friends." A quick look at some of them made it clear that they were frequently signs whose mouth movements resembled those used when pronouncing Swedish words, but those specific words should not (at least not always) be used when translating the signs into Swedish.

It also became increasingly clear to me that for hearing students whose first language is Swedish and who are second-language learners of Swedish Sign Language, a very strong link seems to be created between signs they learn and the Swedish words whose mouth movements the signs are said to be accompanied by. The phrase "are said to be accompanied by" is a key issue here because it is a qualified truth. The link is nevertheless so strong that it will influence the way the learners translate or interpret from Swedish Sign Language into spoken Swedish. They tend to use the Swedish word "seen on the mouth" even when the meaning of the sign might not be well captured by this word, and it will also impede their understanding of the meaning of the sign. The reasons behind the

---

1. The programs I refer to are two year, full-time, sign language programs, whose aim is to teach Swedish Sign Language to persons who want to become sign language interpreters.

creation of this strong link and how it works are interesting and well worth further investigation.

The Use of Glosses

One factor behind the link that seems to be created between a sign and a specific Swedish word might, paradoxically enough, be the fact that Swedish Sign Language, as opposed to Swedish, does not have a written form. When learning Swedish Sign Language, students want to be able to make notes of what they are learning. And teachers want to be able to write single signs as well as whole phrases and sentences on the board during class. A convention of writing Swedish words in capitals to represent signs has evolved in sign language research and has been adopted in sign language teaching as well. The use of only capital letters is supposed to signal that what is seen (and referred to) on the board is not the Swedish word per se, but a sign. (In this volume, all sign language glosses appear in small capital letters.) In this way Swedish words are employed as shorthand glosses for signs. The words are chosen to capture the core meaning of the sign. Sometimes, though, the mouth movement accompanying the sign will influence the choice of word, so in a decision between two Swedish synonyms (or near synonyms), the choice will fall to the one whose mouth movement can be seen, regardless of which is the best translation. At other times one and the same manual sign might be glossed with different words because of the Swedish word that would be used in that context—regardless of the actual mouth movements accompanying the sign. There might even be no mouth movements accompanying the sign at all.

Swedish Mouth Movements?

As is suggested in the quote from *Svenskt teckenspråkslexikon* above, a more detailed analysis reveals that in many cases what is seen is not the mouth pattern of pronouncing a whole Swedish word but rather parts of that word—a reduced form. A sign with "Swedish

mouth movements" may thus be accompanied by a mouth movement resembling the articulation of a whole Swedish word or only
parts of that Swedish word.[2] These word fragments are sometimes
also repeated (during the articulation of a single manual sign), with
the same fragment repeated at least twice, in a way that would result
in nonsense words should the voice be used. The gloss chosen to
represent that sign may still be an ordinary Swedish word, and it
will therefore not reflect the mouth movement required for the
learner to produce the sign correctly. The gloss thus leaves out information that would indicate what the mouth should be doing, and
it might instead contribute to the learner's thinking that mouth
movements of Swedish words accompany these signs, whereas in
fact there are none. There is a strong tendency among students to
see what they expect to see, and the gloss will make them expect to
see the mouth movements of a Swedish word. Any teacher of
Swedish Sign Language will recognize the overuse of complete
Swedish mouth movements as a telltale sign of a beginner.

Let us look closer at two signs in Swedish Sign Language to get
an idea of what happens. There is one sign that means, among other
things, board, as in the board of a company. It is usually glossed
STYRELSE because *styrelse* is the Swedish word for that concept. The
sign is frequently accompanied by a mouth movement, or maybe
more precisely a mouth position, that resembles that of pronouncing the Swedish vowel sound /Y/.[3] But a beginner is very likely to
use the much longer and more complex mouth movement of pronouncing the whole Swedish word. Exactly the same is true for the
sign meaning Germany, *Tyskland* in Swedish, which is glossed TYSK-
LAND. When produced correctly, this sign too should usually be accompanied by the same /Y/, and not the mouth movement of the
whole Swedish word.

---

2. For a thorough discussion and description of mouth movements in Swedish Sign
Language, see Wallin (2002).

3. The symbols used for phonemes are those of the International Phonetic Alphabet. The
exact phonemes are not of major importance here; it is more a question of the number of
phonemes and thus mouth movements.

Non-Swedish Mouth Movements

There are also many signs in Swedish Sign Language that are accompanied by mouth movements that do not resemble the articulation of Swedish words, or fragments of them, at all. These mouth movements, and frequently also the signs themselves, have often been described as "genuine," perhaps because they have been regarded as more genuine to Swedish Sign Language than signs that are accompanied by mouth movements by which "Swedish words" can be seen. These non-Swedish mouth movements can be subdivided into two groups, (1) mouth movements that convey additional linguistic information and (2) mouth movements that are an integral part of the sign but add no extra meaning to it.

Signs accompanied by these so-called genuine mouth movements are sometimes represented by Swedish glosses written in capital letters, despite the lack of Swedish mouth movements. The gloss will often consist of several Swedish words (connected by hyphens) aiming to capture the general meaning of the sign, with no link at all between the mouth movement and the words chosen. Such a gloss will not affect the translation or interpretation of the sign as frequently because it is not connected to the mouth movement of the sign but is chosen to accurately convey the meaning. Actually, I would not be surprised if a frequency count were to show that these words are more frequent in interpreted discourse than in ordinary spoken discourse, though. Sometimes the gloss will be a nonsense word based on the mouth movements seen and an idea of the way a Swedish word would be spelled to result in that mouth movement. These nonsense words will be discussed further below.

Let us again look closer at two signs to get an idea of what we are discussing. There is one sign in Swedish Sign Language that, depending on the context, is often best translated as "just in case," "had better," or something similar. Translating it into Swedish also produces fairly long phrases, not just one word. Usually, though, the sign is represented by the nonsense gloss HYFF, a possible but nonexistent Swedish word that would result in the mouth movement accompanying the sign. The choice of gloss in this case may be linked to the fact that there is no single Swedish word seen on the mouth or used to translate the sign. The other sign I want to discuss as an example of this phenomenon can be translated as "I have no idea," "I don't know," or something similar, with equally long Swedish translations. Here too, the mouth movement has been used to construct a possible Swedish word used as a gloss—ops. The argument for the choice of the gloss HYFF might be true for ops as well. (This sign is interesting also because it is one of the very few signs that are sometimes produced with only the mouth movement and no movement of the hands.) It would seem that nonsense words are no threat to an accurate interpretation of signed discourse; they are not proper words. However, nonsense words like *hyff* and *ops* have actually made their way into the spoken Swedish used by people who are bilingual in Swedish and Swedish Sign Language. Especially in informal situations, it is very easy to let such a "word" slip into the interpretation.

No Standard

As mentioned earlier, the glosses that are used represent only part of the meaning of the sign. A further complicating factor is that the choice and use of them is in no way standardized. Different persons may use the same word as a gloss for different signs, or the same sign may be assigned different glosses depending upon who is doing the glossing. The assigning of glosses that are not based on mouth movements resembling actual Swedish words is not standardized either. A sign that some people gloss BY might be glossed PY by others because the mouth movement for pronouncing those two nonsense syllables is the same.

The Effect on Second-Language Learners

Second-language learners of Swedish Sign Language whose first language is Swedish often have a tendency to see more Swedish mouth movements when they watch a signed discourse than are actually there. This is a tendency that, in my opinion, may actually be reinforced by, or even have its origins in, the use of Swedish words as glosses for signs in sign language teaching.[4] When I ask our students of Swedish Sign Language as a second language which Swedish mouth movements they see in a signed sequence, they frequently overestimate the number of signs accompanied by that kind of mouth movement. Not until we have looked through the sequence several times will they be convinced that many of the signs they claimed had Swedish mouth movements actually did not have them. Sometimes the sign was accompanied by a mouth movement that resembles the pronunciation of only a fragment of the Swedish word whose meaning it more or less shares, and sometimes it was accompanied by a mouth movement not resembling any Swedish word at all but adding linguistic meaning (e.g., an adverbial mouth movement), and sometimes it actually had no mouth movement at all. There are even second-language learners of sign language who believe they *hear* Swedish words when they see a person signing. Looking at somebody (usually a hearing person) signing, they will believe they hear the person whispering, but when they close their eyes, they realize this is not the case.[5]

Signs whose Swedish mouth movements resemble Swedish swearwords or other taboo words constitute a problem of their own. Many second-language learners seem to instinctively avoid the use of mouth movements that "feel like" swearwords in a context in which the students would not ordinarily use such a word. It seems as if second-language learners sometimes have problems separating the two languages—what *feels* like a Swedish swearword (because of the mouth movement accompanying the sign) will also awaken connotations of that Swedish word. The teacher's using that very swearword as a gloss for the sign does not improve the situation, of course. Many long discussions about the differences between the two languages may be required to do away with this erroneous asso-

---

4. The situation truly makes the issue of which came first, the hen or the egg, feel appropriate.
5. Thank you, Inger Ahlgren, for sharing this information with me.

ciation between the mouth movements used in Swedish Sign Language and those used when pronouncing Swedish words.

ENGLISH-SWEDISH FALSE FRIENDS

Ohlander (1997, 342) discusses two main origins of false friends. On the one hand there are misunderstandings or misapprehensions originating in semantic similarity and contextual compatibility in perception; that is, the signs or words in question will have similar meaning and be used in similar contexts and therefore be perceived as having the same meaning. This can in turn lead to incorrect production by the learner. One of his examples is the following word pair: Swedish *eventuellt* and English *eventually*. The actual meaning of the Swedish word is *possibly* or *maybe*. Many Swedish learners of English will mistakenly believe that they understand the meaning of the English word because it looks and sounds so similar to the Swedish word *eventuellt*. Learners will then use *eventually* when in fact *possibly* or *maybe* would be the correct choice.

On the other hand, according to Ohlander, there are words with only a very striking formal similarity. Two words look or sound the same despite a lack of semantic similarity and contextual compatibility, yet their similarity can lead to a mistaken idea that the two words have identical meaning. One of his examples is the following word pair: Swedish *freestyle* and English *freestyle*. The actual meaning of the Swedish word is *Walkman*. I have frequently heard fellow Swedes (speaking English) talk about their freestyle when they were in fact talking about their *Walkman*. A further source of confusion in this case is that the so-called Swedish word is a word whose structure is clearly English and not Swedish, giving true cause to wonder why it ever came to be the "Swedish" word for the concept. It would be possible to conduct a similar discussion regarding the words and signs we discuss here.[6]

---

6. I will, however, refrain from doing so, in order to avoid the problems of mixing even more languages, one of which has no written form.

In the earlier-mentioned *English Synonyms and False Friends*, the authors use another, more pragmatic, definition of the concept of false friends:

> As for *False Friends* we have only included ones that we know are easily confused by Swedes, and not taken any notice of pseudo-problems such as "crop—kropp," which in practice do not cause any difficulties. (Hargevik and Stevens 1987, 3, my translation)

The authors here refrain from accounting for certain words that according to their earlier, stricter, definition would constitute false friends, claiming that in practice, they do not create any problems. We are thus faced with word pairs that could cause trouble but don't, as well as word pairs that do. Ohlander (1997, 333–34) also states that the demands for formal and semantic similarity will result in designating exactly the kind of word pairs that never, or very infrequently, cause problems or are mistaken for each other as false friends. According to him, if you want to find the words that actually do create problems for a learner, you might do better focusing not only on words with formal similarities (i.e., words that look or sound similar) but on words whose meanings lie within the same fairly narrow semantic field as well. One of his examples is the word pair Swedish *novell* and English *novel*; the meaning of the Swedish word *novell* is actually *short story*. Many Swedish beginners of English do believe that *novel* means *short story*.

SIGN LANGUAGE LEARNERS' PROBLEMS

Ohlander (1997) also discusses the risk of the learner's using words that are plausible analogical formations but that actually do not exist in the language being learned. The Swedish-speaking learner of Swedish Sign Language is in trouble here too. Beginners find it easy to continue thinking in their native language (especially with a whole board full of linguistic symbols belonging to that language) and come up with a construction they think is a possible sign language construction. If they use it, they may be understood because most deaf teachers of sign language know Swedish, and the students may labor under the misapprehension that what they produced was correct.

Another problem caused by the use of Swedish words as glosses for signs is that a second-language learner may easily develop the misapprehension that the sign and the word have exactly the same meaning.

LANGUAGE PROFICIENCY AND FALSE FRIENDS

In general it can be said that the degree of language proficiency, and to some extent the amount of knowledge about the culture of the language you are learning, will decide which words and signs actually create problems and which do not. As the language skills in the new language increase, the number of potential and actual false friends decreases. This is true also for the language pair of Swedish Sign Language and Swedish, but with one possible and important exception. Because the linguistic symbols of the one (words) are used as glosses for the linguistic symbols of the other (signs), the two languages are constantly used together. This is quite likely to affect the learner's ability to keep the two languages distinct.[7]

WHAT ABOUT INTERPRETING?

Where does the teaching of sign language interpreting enter the picture? Based on my research, I find strong indications that the links created between certain pairs of signs and words, especially when learning sign language as a second language, create problems for interpreters. There may be incorrect assumptions on the interpreter's side regarding the meaning of a sign (based on the meaning of the word used as a gloss to represent it). The mouth movements that are a part of the correct production of some signs also seem to

---

7. I will completely avoid the whole complex issue that Swedish Sign Language is a minority language (without a written form) submerged in the majority context of Swedish in its written form.

cause interpreters—almost automatically and without reflection—to use the words these mouth movements remind them of. During simultaneous interpreting the interpreter is constantly under pressure to produce an accurate and appropriate message while pressed for time. Although the interpreter is probably aware of a sign's having many different meanings, it is very likely that either the Swedish word "seen" on the mouth of the signer or the Swedish word used as a gloss for the sign will be the word that first comes to the interpreter's mind—and is produced in the interpretation. The result can be unidiomatic and monotonous language use, as well as an interpretation lacking in equivalence regarding both linguistic style and semantic content.

In my work with interpreting students, I have therefore focused on their awareness of language use in different contexts. I have used exercises in which students practice finding synonyms in both languages, exercises to make them sensitive to what is correct language usage in both languages, exercises to make them aware of some of the most important (i.e., frequent) false friends in the language pair of Swedish Sign Language and spoken Swedish, and so on.

SOME SUGGESTIONS FOR EXERCISES

It is important that students become aware of these treacherous false friends at a very early stage in their learning of sign language and that this awareness then be heightened during interpreting training. They will need both to be on the lookout for false friends and to learn to think of as many synonyms as possible for words and for signs.

The whole issue of whether to use words from the national spoken language as glosses or not is a complicated one, which I have only touched upon but which deserves further consideration. Addressing groups of sign language students or interpreting students, I realized it was very easy to make them all say the same word in chorus by just showing them a sign and asking them to say the first Swedish word that came to mind. To have students do this and then to point out to them what happens will give them a first indication of the strength of this connection between signs and words. The next step is to ask them to come up with as many other words as possible that could be used instead. A continuation of this exercise is to discuss the context in which each word would be suitable.

When I visited the training program for conference interpreters at the Sorbonne in Paris, France, the students had special interpreting classes in which they were instructed to avoid at all costs so-called cognates, that is, words that are related to each other (due to the languages being related to each other) and sound similar. It is possible to do a similar exercise with sign-language-interpreting students, telling them they must never use the word used as a gloss for the sign or seen on the mouth. The next step here can be to soften up a bit and allow the use of these words if, and only if, the students have solid arguments for what they are doing.

Another way of making students aware of false friends is to work between different linguistic registers. In Swedish Sign Language, signs with Swedish mouth movements have a tendency to be more frequent in a more formal register, something the students need to be made aware of. It is possible to work from a short written text (e.g., a news item) and ask them to change it into a different register (e.g., tell it as if it were something they have experienced themselves). This exercise can also be done the other way around—take something a student has experienced and make a news item out of it. The whole point is linguistic sensitivity and linguistic awareness.

Linguistic awareness regarding the correctness of Swedish taboo words on the mouth in Swedish Sign Language, and the correct interpretation of them into spoken Swedish, is also important. It is essential that the students look at a large variety of sign language texts with the express aim of identifying signs whose math movements look like swearwords or other taboo words. The texts should of course be picked precisely because they contain this specific linguistic feature. When these signs have been identified, students should discuss the style, correctness, and other features of this usage in the text. The next step is to go on to discuss what would constitute an equivalent translation into spoken language in that context.

A different area of language use, which is also of interest, is how people are addressed and referred to in various situations. In Swedish Sign Language most name signs are accompanied by the mouth movements of only part of the person's name. Frequently it is the first name, but sometimes it is the last name. Name signs accompanied by both the first and the last name of the person are very infrequent. Someone can be introduced or discussed using the name sign only, even in quite formal settings. In spoken Swedish, though, it would be considered rude to use only part of a person's name when introducing or discussing the person in the corresponding settings. Especially the use of only the first name would be considered much too familiar. If the interpreter is not aware of this difference and uses only part of the name, the interpretation will be in the wrong register and might actually cause offense when none was intended. The part of the name that is pronounced in the spoken interpretation tends to be the part of the name that can be seen on the mouth. Finding exercises that make students aware of this issue entails gathering examples of appropriate situations (from taped sessions of the National Associations of the Deaf or other large organizations, television programs, etc.), showing them, and discussing them in class. Working from these video recordings in interpreting classes will also make students remember that name signs are actually a kind of false friend when it comes to language register.

Greeting an audience in a formal setting such as an annual general meeting in a large organization, a public lecture, or similar meeting is also a situation in which language usage differs between Swedish Sign Language and spoken Swedish. Whereas a person using Swedish Sign Language will use a greeting that unwittingly might be translated as "Hi, everybody!" or something similar, a person speaking Swedish will use a much more formal greeting or no greeting at all before commencing the speech. If we want students to make an accurate interpretation of the greeting phrase from Swedish Sign Language into spoken Swedish, we have to make sure they are aware of the differences in register used and make them practice greeting phrases in different settings in both languages. Needless to say, there are many more settings in which students need to be made aware of, and practice using, the set phrases used in both languages.

CONCLUSION

False friends are one important concept to take into consideration when training interpreters. Other areas that have been touched upon in the chapter are of equal importance, although it is my firm belief that the very nature of sign language teaching and the relationship between the spoken and the sign languages of a country are factors that make the false friends in such a language pair extra false.

As mentioned earlier, linguistic awareness and extensive knowledge of the two working languages are essential tools for the working interpreter. The general aim of all the suggested exercises is to make students aware that using the word that first comes to mind, because it is used as a gloss for the sign or because they think they can "see" it, will keep the interpretation on a word-for-word level instead of the meaning-based level we strive for. In addition to this linguistic awareness, constant discussions regarding idiomatic language usage in the two working languages, as well as the changes and developments in the languages, are a necessity for all interpreters, new and old.

ACKNOWLEDGMENTS

I would like to take the opportunity to thank all colleagues and students who have willingly discussed this issue with me, thereby increasing my knowledge of the subject. A warm thank-you also goes to Cynthia Roy for insightful comments on an earlier version of this chapter and for keeping a lookout on my English.

REFERENCES

Hargevik, S., and M. Stevens. 1978. *English synonyms and false friends.* Liber Läromedel: Malmö.

Ohlander, S. 1997. *Prolegomena till en teori om falsk vänskap.* In: A.-B. Andersson, I. Enström, R. Källström, K. Nauclér (red.), Svenska som andraspråk och andra språk. Festskrift till Gunnar Tingbjörn. Inst. för svenska språket, Göteborgs universitet, 329–45.

Svenskt teckenspråkslexikon. 1997. Sveriges Dövas Riksförbund: Leksand.

Trask, R. L. 1993. *A dictionary of grammatical terms in linguistics.* London: Routledge.

Wallin, L. 2002. Two kinds of productive signs in Swedish Sign Language: Polysynthetic signs and size and shape specifying signs. *Sign Language and Linguistics* 3 (2):237–56.

KYRA POLLITT AND CLAIRE HADDON
WITH THE INTERPRETING TEAM OF
THE UNIVERSITY OF CENTRAL
LANCASHIRE, ENGLAND, U.K.

Cold Calling? Retraining Interpreters in the Art of Telephone Interpreting

THE TELEPHONE IS an instrument of culture(s) based on sound and as such is foreign to Deaf communities. Interpreted telephone interaction, in which all three participants are not physically present and cannot see each other, is conducted through the medium of sound, a medium that is culturally comfortable for the participants who can hear, which usually includes the interpreter.[1]

This chapter describes training activities that challenge assumptions and practices that have developed around interpreted telephone interaction. It questions whether a fresh approach to this type of interpreting might be more politically liberating for Deaf people and more comfortable for all participants involved.

Although not specifically designed for video-interpreted interaction, these thoughts and exercises are applicable to any instance in which the three participants, Deaf and hearing persons and an interpreter, do not share simultaneous visual contact.

---

1. Because this chapter describes telephone interpreting, the word *interpreter* will refer to hearing interpreters working between signed and spoken languages. Should any readers know of instances in which similar work is being undertaken by Deaf interpreters, the authors would be most grateful for further information.

RATIONALE

CAN YOU MAKE A PHONE CALL FOR ME? has long been a familiar refrain in Deaf/hearing circles. Telecommunications are a huge part of our postmodern, technological life experience, and although faxes, e-mail, text messaging (SMS), and the development of text-phone relay services are all liberating forms of communication that enable Deaf and hearing people to interact directly, they do not yet reach into every corner of society and satisfy every telecommunicative purpose. At the same time, the use of the telephone for the provision of services is spreading; it is now possible to use the phone to arrange a mortgage, order flowers for a loved one, have a medical consultation, transfer money between bank accounts, and so on; the list is almost endless.

For Deaf people it is still often the case that the most convenient and expedient way of accessing this world of remote services is via an interpreter. Thus interpreters increasingly find that telephone work focuses on what Cheepen (2000) terms *transactional* phone calls. For both caller and interpreter, these calls may involve negotiating switchboard operators, answering machines, mechanized option menus, and other complexities before the real business of talk even begins.

To make matters worse, the fact that not all participants are face-to-face (even in videophone interpreting) has an enormous effect on the dynamics of the exchange. The nature of sign languages demands that the interpreter be either present or visible to the Deaf participant via a video screen. The other participant often has no visual access to either the interpreter or the Deaf person. Therefore, because the Deaf person can see the interpreter, these two will expect things to operate according to the usual norms of working together, and the third person, having only sound as a guide, will expect the norms of telephone interaction to apply. Thus cross-cultural considerations and issues of power and representation assume heightened significance.

In an interpreted telephone interaction, then, what do interpreters aim to do and how do they hope to do it? Without a clear ideological and practical framework, the interpreter often feels forced to choose sides; for example, in the awkward pause, does the interpreter fill in the gaps or focus on the Deaf person? Telephone interpreting is highly complex work, and one may have grounds for claiming that it is among the most complicated that any interpreter working between signed and spoken languages may face. Yet in the United Kingdom, telephone interpreting is a Cinderella among interpreting domains, rarely specifically taught in training courses. It is assumed that interpreters will simply apply what theories they have learned—after all, this is basically triadic interpreting, isn't it?

It is our experience that even interpreters who have been trained at the most progressive institutions and are well versed in the likes of Skopostheorie (for a succinct account, see Vermeer 1989) somehow seem to revert to a conduit approach at the drop of a ringtone. The justification often cited for this behavior is that the interpreter is seeking to empower the Deaf person and give him or her control of the exchange. Yet surely control can be achieved only if the interaction is successful. Is anyone in control of an interaction that confuses all participants? In fact, research into telephone talk among regular users indicates that in transactional exchanges, it is expected that the caller will be conversationally subservient to the agent (the professional telephone user). What's more, much of the delicate social interaction that frames successful transactions via telephone revolves around this central tenet (for more on these issues, see Cheepen 2000).

Let's start with a real-life example. One day, one of us happened to be in a familiar work environment, one in which Deaf and hearing people had been working together as equal members of a team for a number of years. It was the beginning of the working day, and one of the hearing team members (let's call him Gerry) was checking his answering machine messages. One of the messages was from a woman. She said, "Hi, it's David here. I'm sorry I'm not going to be able to make it into the office today. My wife's really sick. Would you mind phoning up to Personnel for me?" Gerry's reaction was interesting. Gerry did a double take. He rewound the answering machine and said, "What on earth was that?" It was only when he played the message again that he realized that this was, of course, an interpreted message, spoken by an interpreter whose voice he easily recognized, on behalf of his friend and colleague of many years, David.

Perhaps you are thinking that Gerry should have known that this was an interpreted call. Well, he did . . . eventually. His first instinct upon listening to a telephone message, though, was to seek clues from the caller's voice and the structure of the talk, not the content of the call.

Perhaps you are thinking that David was at fault because he failed to explain clearly at the beginning of the call that he was speaking via an interpreter. Yet it is possible, conversely, that to do so would only have deepened Gerry's confusion by adding another layer of complication to the message, removing it even further from the conventions and norms of telephone talk.

The exercises described below aim to increase awareness of the complexity of interpreted telephone interaction, highlighting some of the factors and dynamics involved and suggesting ways to encourage interpreting students to develop new frameworks and approaches that will enable new scripts for facilitating telephone interaction.

USING THIS EQUIPMENT

The material reproduced here charts a process of teaching and learning. We think this is a flexible process that can be used equally effectively with novice interpreters and with the very experienced. It is also a training package that works well with groups of mixed experience and ability (as ours was).

The process as presented here can be adapted to suit an intensive training event taking place over a number of days or to a series of sessions taking place over a number of weeks. We have provided suggestions for classroom activities at each stage of the process but would encourage trainers to be flexible in adapting the ideas and materials to meet the needs of their participants (we are great believers in the "learner-led" approach) and the wider societies in which they will be working (many of our examples come from Great Britain and British English).

"HOLD THE LINE, PLEASE"

Most of the interpreters undertaking this training will already have had some experience with interpreting telephone calls (hence the *retraining* in the title). This is as true for newcomers to Deaf communities as it is for children of Deaf adults. Many will consider that they can "do" telephone interpreting and that there is little to learn in regard to this domain.

Many may also be aware that literature is available on telephone interpreting between spoken and signed languages. The first part of the process, then, is a critical literature review. Here students should develop an understanding of the evolution of ideas and practices by examining, chronologically, the literature on telephone interpreting. Students should also be encouraged to begin to critique and challenge conventional wisdom by reference to their own practices.

Suggested Activities

The trainer should review the literature and present a synopsis of the development of ideas and practices. Throughout, the trainer should encourage participants to engage critically with the material presented and to relate it to the students' own practices. The example given here is, of course, drastically compressed, and trainers should seek to give as broad a review as possible. So, for example, the trainer might present something like the following:

> Back in 1981, Sharon Neuman-Solow was recommending that interpreters should always use the first person when telephone interpreting so that "the interpreter signs what is said and vocalises signs, using the first person so that the two clients talk to one another directly" (74).

The trainer might then ask the group to share any experiences when using the first person has been particularly successful and some when it has been particularly unsuccessful.

The trainer may wish to keep a tally of successful and unsuccessful anecdotes on a board or flip chart. Alternatively, participants can undertake this tally as a personal reflection exercise, sharing the results with the group.

> Mindess (1991) suggested that it may be better for the Deaf person to concentrate on the content of the call, not the form (because the form is structured for those who can hear). Metzger (1999) began to think about applying this notion, saying "Providing no introduction of an interpreter can leave participants feeling confused about who to talk to and how the interaction should proceed. . . . Who should be responsible for such introductions and how they might best be carried out is an area for further investigation."

The trainer might ask students what Mindess's suggestion could look like in practice or how to answer the question that Metzger poses. As the literature under critical review becomes more current, the discussion should begin to connect to the next stage of the process (see below).

The trainer should allocate a book or article to each participant and assign a short presentation, to be given to the whole group, of the ideas and practices described therein. This works well as a precourse activity.

Participants should then be invited to engage in critical debate in which they are prompted to evaluate these theories by relating them to their own practical successes and failures. This debate should be facilitated by the trainer because it is important to foster an honest and supportive environment in which criticism is mutual and constructive.

By the end of this phase, participants should have become aware of a range of issues in relation to telephone interpreting. The particular range will depend on the literature that the trainer has chosen, but trainers should aim to have raised at least the following points:

• issues surrounding role (using first person versus reported speech; introducing the interpreter; establishing who is in control when dialing or handling operators, answering machines, and other equipment)
• issues of empowerment (whether the Deaf and hearing participants have equal control, how powerful the interpreter is perceived to be, etc.)
• issues of talk (dealing with interruptions, cross-talk, silences, laughter, pauses, phatics,[2] reflecting the mood, etc.)

Some useful readings include but are not limited to Dickinson (2002), Frishberg (1986), Mindess (1991), Metzger (1999), Neuman-Solow (1981), Timm (2000), and Wadensjö (1999). By no means exhaustive, this list is included to provide a starting point for trainers to build on.

COULD YOU REPEAT THAT?

Now that students have begun to deconstruct theoretically the act of interpreting telephone interaction, it is necessary to reinforce this increased awareness by applying these critiques to real practices. This part of the process involves fun, practical activities that highlight the flaws of accepted practices to participants. For these exercises to succeed, participants need to be honest about their actual practices (not what they wish they could do nor what they think they should do if someone is checking up on them). They also need to be comfortable with each other and with the learning environ-

---

2. We are here using *phatic* in a Malinowskian sense of speech communication used to establish social relationships rather than to impart information. See Malinowski, B. 1923. The problem of meaning in primitive languages. In *The meaning of meaning*, ed. C. Ogden and I. A. Richards, 146-52. London: Routledge and Kegan Paul.

ment. When this is not the case, trainers may wish to consider team-building exercises before undertaking such activities.

Suggested Activities

Working as a whole group, participants take turns to volunteer a typical example of their telephone interpreting practice. The trainer takes the role of devil's advocate, critiquing and deconstructing the students' practices from the perspective of the other participants in the interaction.

Working in groups of three, participants each take on the roles of Deaf person, interpreter, and hearing person. The "Deaf person" and the "interpreter" should sit together with their backs to the "hearing person." The "Deaf person" and "interpreter" then act out a telephone call that the "Deaf person" is instigating (it is useful for the trainer to fix a purpose for the imaginary call, such as a call to a college concerning enrollment). The "hearing person" must play devil's advocate, highlighting the unnatural aspects of the exchange. Each participant should have a turn at playing each role.

Alternatively, the trainer can engage the services of a number of people who can hear and are not used to interpreted telephone interaction. The exercise described above is repeated, and the trainer or group asks the invited guests for their feedback on how they felt during the conversation. This approach, although helpful, denies students the valuable experience of role-playing as the hearing person.

If trainers use this approach, they need to brief the hearing guests on providing constructive feedback. As a guide, here are some example comments from previous training sessions. Due to the constraints of reproduction in this format, we have included only the interpreter's voice (I) and the hearing person's comments (H.P.'s comments).

I: "Hi, it's John Jones here, calling through an interpreter . . ."

H.P.'s comments: "I've got lots of problems here. What's an interpreter? I thought they were for people who spoke other languages, but I can't hear any other voices on the line. This person's voice sounds cold and funny, and their talk is too slow."

I: "Hi, I'm an interpreter phoning on behalf of John Jones . . ."

H.P.'s comments: "This sounds like a sales pitch. Why are you phoning on behalf of someone else? Either you are selling me something or you are up to no good. I feel suspicious. Is the other person even there? Are you some kind of criminal or some kind of helper?"

I: "Hello, my name is Sally Smith and I've got John Jones with me. He is Deaf. Hello, I want to ask you about . . ."

H.P.'s comments: "The introduction bit felt fine, though you could wonder why someone on the phone was telling you who they were with! It was confusing to figure out who was talking to me later on, though. I thought that I was dealing with a lady called Sally, then figured out that she had switched to being John Jones, but she still sounded like Sally!"

Loud and Clear!

By now participants should be sensitized to the telephone environment and its complexities, and they will also be beginning to consider the hearing person's perspective of the interpreted call. Further work is now required on understanding listening and talking in telephone interaction.

The next phase, then, is actually to listen to hearing telephone calls. As telephone users themselves, interpreters have a great deal of knowledge about how telephone talk works. The problem is that this knowledge is so embedded in our behavior that it is often difficult to make it explicit. Much of the frustration interpreters feel when undertaking telephone work arises from the fact that they often have to override their instincts because they are bound by other considerations.

At this point in the process, trainers need to make participants aware of their own natural behaviors as telephone users. This work needs to be guided, and it is useful to begin by making some of the distinctions that are found in the literature. It is no coincidence that the factors highlighted by linguists are precisely those interpreters identify as some of the most difficult to deal with.

The first useful distinction to make is between telephone calls that are conversational and those that are transactional (see Cheepen 2000 for some good definitions). Transactional calls can be further divided into those that take place between the caller and a human agent and those that involve interaction with machine-generated talk, such as options menus.

It is important to stress to participants that it is highly unlikely that any telephone call will be entirely transactional or conversational; there are often elements of transaction in our personal calls, and businesses will often train staff or program machinery to conversationalize business calls, thinking customers experience such calls as more user-friendly (see Fairclough 1995 for more on the conversationalization of public discourses).

Further, it is useful to focus on certain conventionalized aspects of telephone talk. The most frequently considered, by linguists and interpreters alike, are openings, confirmations, and closings. In the literature these categories are further subdivided. Although it is useful to bring these subdivisions to the attention of participants, the subcategories may introduce too much complexity at this stage.

If the training is taking place over a number of sessions, trainers will be able to make use of both of the exercises outlined for this part of the process. The exercises can be used in the order in which they appear here, which has the effect of allowing participants to become aware of what they are hearing or saying before they further analyze its meanings. They can also be used in the reverse order, however, when the analysis activity needs to be based on data provided by the trainer. In this case the exercise gives participants a clear framework for the collection of their own data but tends to focus the listening activity on certain features.

If the structure of the training event does not allow time for the first activity, trainers should focus on the second activity as a classroom exercise, with the trainer undertaking the first activity as preparation and to provide data for the classroom work—unless the trainer has access to some excellent equipment and a corpus of telephone call data. Alternatively, the second activity can be set as a postcourse continuation exercise (indeed, students should be encouraged to undertake such activities as part of their own long-term personal development).

Suggested Activities

Students should fill in table 1 with examples of talk from their own personal (i.e., not interpreted) telephone exchanges. These should be brought back to the group and the information shared. At this point the trainer may wish to reintroduce or reinforce further categorization of the data (e.g., by subdividing the confirmation category into channel checking, discourse monitoring, or information verification). Participants should be encouraged to reflect on the increased awareness that comes from this activity. Trainers should anticipate that participants may have had difficulty categorizing some of their talk; this is usually evidence of the "conversationalization" mentioned above. The data produced by the participants can then be used for the next exercise.

To really understand what is happening in these telephone exchanges, we need to get down to the nitty-gritty and make our listening and talking expertise explicit. To do this we need to take a real hard look at what words we are using and hearing and what effect they have on the exchanges we are involved in. We know of no better tool for this than critical discourse analysis (Fairclough 1995). More flexible and less technical than other forms of discourse analysis, this is something that everyday interpreters can grasp quickly and use easily (see also Pollitt 2000).

This example, taken from Cheepen (2000, 294), is a brief critical discourse analysis of an opening and an example of the discussion trainers might have with students.

Table 1. Data Gathering

	Openings	Confirmations	Closings
Conversational			
Transactional (human)			
Transactional (machine)			

"Blankshire Electricity, Mary Smith speaking—how may I help you?"

Critical Discourse Analysis
The first section "Blankshire Electricity" is purely transactional. It functions to tell the caller which service they are connected to. The second section "Mary Smith speaking" (which is not used by all call centres) is both transactional and interactional. It signals to the caller that the agent is, in a sense, the "right" person to talk to—i.e., someone who can probably answer questions and deal with problems on their own authority and initiative, as opposed to, say, a switchboard operator, who can only forward the call to some more senior figure. An additional transactional function here is to give the caller sufficiently detailed information to be able to call again and ask for the same person if a problem should arise. There is also, however, an interactional function in the announcement of the agent's name—which is the underlining of the human-ness of that agent.

In addition to this there is also an aspect of this section which communicates to the caller what we can think of as a kind of textual meaning related to the expected pattern of the dialogue which will ensue. It indicates, in fact, that the dialogue may be fairly lengthy and complex. If the expectation by the service provider was that the dialogue would be brief and simple then there would be little advantage to the agent giving her name. When the agent does give her name she is signalling that she is trained for and prepared to participate in a dialogue of some complexity.

The third section of the opening—"how may I help you?" is a formulaic structure which signals the transactional function "you may ask me questions" and also "I am in a position to answer them." It also functions textually, by using an interrogative form, which both requires an answer and simultaneously hands the next turn at talk to the caller . . . Ritualised politeness is clearly communicated by this formula, and some directly interpersonal material is also included in the form of the personal pronouns "I" and "you" so, as with the announcement of the agent's name, we see the flavour of small talk in this formulaic catering for the human-ness of the dialogue participants.

These activities enable students to become much more aware of the complexity and ritual of telephone interaction. They should be aware of the features and importance of politeness and friendliness in telephone talk and of how we recognize and use a variety of tiny signals to give and concede authority, give permission, and show friendliness, support, approval, and disapproval; how we manipulate pauses and silences to appear kind or harsh; and how we use certain words to signal and re-signal imminent closure (Cheepen [2000] even comments that this signaling can be so rhythmic that it sounds almost like a round song), ensuring that everyone has signaled acceptance of closure before final completion of the talk.

Suggested Readings

Some useful readings include Aijmer (1996), Cheepen, (2000), Clark and French (1981), Fairclough (1995), Hopper (1989), Luke and Pavlidou (2002), and Pollitt (2000).

How Can We Help You?

Professional telephone users, such as those who work in call centers or telesales, are trained to understand telephone talk and ritual and manipulate it to their advantage, creating the precise dialogue effect that suits them best. Although we are not advocating that interpreters should sound like telesales representatives, our practices can benefit from an insight into how other telephone professionals are trained.

If we are to function effectively as mediators of telephone interaction, it is important that we understand not only Deaf people's alienation and their response to taking or relinquishing control, as well as the expectations and assumptions surrounding telephone talk, but also the ways professionals are expected to interact on the phone.

The next activity in this sequence should simply be to expose interpreters to the kind of training that professional telephone users receive. Many materials are available on video, and it is worth searching the Internet or contacting local call centers to locate them.

Trainers should pay particular attention to finding resources local to them because, for example, British English telephone talk norms differ in some regards from those of other forms of English, such as American English. The following, therefore, represent just a sample of the materials available: Honey (1986), Whalen and Henderson (2002), and Video Arts (1986).

Tell You Later?

At this stage of the process, students have critically re-evaluated the literature on telephone interpreting between signed and spoken languages and reflected on their own practices and those of their colleagues, they have considered how telephone interaction might be perceived by people who are not accustomed to interpreters, and they have examined the norms of telephone talk and the ways professional telephone users manipulate those norms. It is now time to re-evaluate interpreted telephone interaction from the perspective of the Deaf participant.

In typical interpreted interaction, Deaf people can see not only the interpreter but all other participants with whom they seek to interact. The metanotative elements of the speech-sign interpretation can, therefore, be measured against the facial expressions and body language of the original speaker and whatever sounds the Deaf person may be able to pick up. Similarly, when the interpreter is working from a sign language to a spoken language, the Deaf person may not be able to access the metanotative qualities of sound that the interpreter is employing to represent the mood and tone of that Deaf person's utterances but is able to judge the reaction of the other participant to the interpreter's spoken message. None of these cues are possible in telephone interaction. This lack represents a disempowerment of the Deaf person.

How, then, might interpreters compensate for this lack? Many Deaf people seek to increase their control of the interaction. This is a common although, we argue, misguided response. We have already noted that spoken telephone interaction is deeply ritualized and intensely complex, with metanotative vocal qualities and phatic responses assuming inordinate significance. How reasonable is it, then, that Deaf people can control an interaction that relies on such sound-dependent expectations and assumptions?

It is also common for an interpreter and a Deaf person to collude in seeking to create an interpretation that seeks to "project a Utopian community that is not yet realized" (Venuti 2000, 485). In pretending that the person at one end of the telephone is exactly the same (in interactional terms) as the person at the other end, and therefore that the conversation can proceed as any other, interpreters not only create a false utopia (because signed and spoken languages *are* different), we negate Deaf identities and Deaf cultures by attempting to assimilate them to the values and norms of spoken-language cultures.

WHO'S AFRAID OF THE BIG, BAD S/HE?

The most common tool in creating unrealized utopias in telephone interaction is the insistence by many interpreters on the use of the first person to reflect the utterances of the Deaf person. This insistence ushers in many problems. Students will have noted from

earlier examples and exercises that telephone users are easily confused by the interpreter's use of first person to refer to the other primary participant. In addition, this form of conduit-style interpretation places an onus on the interpreter to attempt to reflect all the
metanotative and phatic qualities that are so important to telephone
talk. In simultaneous interpretation between signed and spoken languages, in which *décalage* (time lag) is marked not by the noise of a
foreign language being spoken but by silence, the interpreter is faced
with an impossible task. Any silences or pauses created by *décalage*
will be afforded significance by other telephone users. So talk from
the Deaf person will be perceived as odd by the person who can
hear, that person remains confused as to who is being addressed,
and the interpreter is unable to achieve a successful interpretation.

Venuti (1998) has argued that this ideology of the invisible interpreter who seeks to create a false utopia wherein all interactants
are equal and assimilated can easily be challenged by "foreignizing," a process in which the act of translation or interpretation
is rendered more apparent, highlighting the cultural and linguistic
differences between the parties. Discussing translation rather than
interpretation, he suggests that translators consider rendering certain textual elements (culturally weighted lexical items, certain idioms that afford cultural insight, or even particular syntactic structures) in a way that marks them as different from the linguistic
norms of the second language. This method has the advantage of
disempowering the interpreter in favor of the other participants;
when such items are marked, participants are able to question the
real meaning of a term or phrase and thereby explore and experience the culture of the other for themselves.

Widespread attitudes to deafness as a disability, however, mean
the interpreter working between signed and spoken languages must
be more cautious in employing this approach. Llewellyn-Jones
(1981) noted the effect of the unconscious and uncontrolled "foreignizing" of sign-to-speech texts on the judgments of audiences
who were not Deaf. It remains true that, even judging on the basis
of a consciously and carefully "foreignized" rendition of signed

terms into spoken languages, hearing people are less likely to assume that, say, a French speaker is retarded or somehow a deficient version of themselves.

Textual foreignizing, we would urge, should be employed with caution and seldom on the phone when working between signed and spoken languages. There are, however, other means to render the act of interpretation more apparent and thus alert both parties to the cultural differences that abound between Deaf and hearing people. The simplest means is by bringing the mediated nature of the exchange to the fore. Conveniently, there are a number of established means of achieving this on the phone, most notable of which is the interpreter as operator. As Dickinson (2002) points out, although interpreted calls can never be as "natural" as direct telephone talk, we cannot expect to have our own set of rules; we have to fit into existing ones as best we can. The role of operator is one that is familiar and comfortable to the hearing person, permits the interpreter greater flexibility of role (using third person and reported speech or action), and allows the Deaf person to assert his or her identity as a Deaf person.

Just Connecting You Now

In this phase of the process, we begin to think about what effect our newfound knowledge and awareness should have on our practices. If the interpreter is mediator (see Wadensjö 1999), how can this mediation be most effectively achieved? What ideological frameworks are we adopting, and where are the boundaries of our practice? Can telephone interpreting ever be conduit interpreting (for example if the interaction is with machine-generated talk)? What alternatives are there to the conduit model?

We are not advocating here that telephone interpreting must always be conducted in a particular way. As Mindess (1991, 163) has suggested, we need "a closet full of models" for each and every interpreting task, and telephone interpreting is no exception. The requirements of interpretation will differ not only according to the type of telephone interaction being interpreted but according to the Deaf and hearing people involved and the unfolding relationships between the Deaf person, the hearing person, and the interpreter as the interaction progresses.

Suggested Activity

This next task can be either a whole-group activity (say a maximum of ten participants) or a small-group exercise (three participants per group is ideal). Using the same categories as earlier (conversational and transactional; openings, confirmations, and closings), try to generate scripts that are appropriate to interpreted telephone interactions.

With students working in smaller groups, encourage them to try out these scripts by electing a member of the group to be the hearing participant, one to be the interpreter, and one to be an objective observer. The hearing participant and objective observer should comment on the advantages and disadvantages of the scripts. Rotate the roleplay so that each participant has at least one turn in each role.

With students working in a larger group, the scripts should be constructed by the group, and the trainer should take the role of critic.

Trainers should ensure that scripts consider the following factors:

- *décalage*
- phatics
- reporting action, laughter, or other signals
- the appropriate use of first or third person and how to signal any transition between the two (consider here that we may already signal reported speech in our signed interpretations by tilt of the head or eye gaze)
- signaling turn-taking
- the merits of consecutive versus simultaneous interpreting

- cross-talk (remember that cross-talk is often a positive attribute of spoken discourse, signaling support, agreement, or approval to the speaker)
- interruptions
- the interpreter's relationship to the listener
- the interpreter's relationship to the signer
- other means of communication (for example, having a pencil and paper at hand can be useful, particularly when encountering automated menu options)
- whether all participants have the right to know who is present and that their contributions are being interpreted

An Example of Students' Work

Figure 1 is a sample "formula" devised by educational interpreters at the University of Central Lancashire who were working on scripts for openings in transactional (human) telephone discourses between University staff members, together with some notes the group came up with for dealing with difficulties not covered by the formula. This work was generated entirely within the training session.

The Students' Notes

How to stop a Deaf person from interrupting or overlapping:

- break eye contact
- look at the phone to indicate the person on the other end is still speaking
- use "hold" handshape (makes it clear things are not finished yet)
- could try "Ok, John is still signing, but I'm going to have to stop you both and clarify. Lucy, can you repeat what you just said? . . . Ok, John's response is coming now . . . (then back to first person)

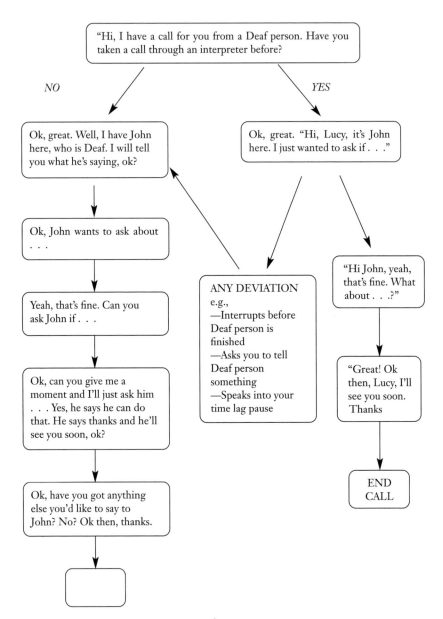

Figure 1. Students' flow chart for interpreted intrauniversity transactional telephone talk

How to stop a hearing person from interrupting or overlapping: in the case of hearing people interrupting because of silences, go into operator mode; for example, "Sorry to keep you waiting."

The Future Is Bright

Although students should by now have experienced an increase in awareness and sensitivity to the complexities and demands of telephone interpreting, it is important to remember that as interpreters, we are not working in a vacuum. Although we have had the privilege of opportunity to reflect, analyze, debate, and create, users of our services may not. This process of learning may lead students to adapt their practices and to deviate from established methods of working with Deaf and hearing people.

Retrained interpreters need to be aware of the issues involved in changing their practices and sensitive to the concerns of the other participants.

Before interpreters leave the training program, it is useful for them to discuss and exchange ideas about how to introduce and negotiate these changes with communities of both Deaf and hearing users of interpreting services.

Suggested Activity

Students should be divided into groups according to whether group members work in similar circumstances. The concerns of interpreters who work within organizations that have a relatively stable constituency of Deaf and hearing people will differ from those whose work serves a diverse and changeable freelance market.

This discursive exercise provides an opportunity for participants to reflect on how they will translate their new knowledge and awareness into their working practices. The focus should be on strategies for implementation (such as setting up a workshop to train Deaf and hearing colleagues in what to expect from interpreted telephone interaction or developing a checklist for preparatory discussion with Deaf people who request telephone interpreting services).

Students should be encouraged to write down at least two action points to take away with them. Trainers should ensure they either have a copy of these points or facilitate the exchange of contact details between students. The program can then include a follow-up discussion (after, say, two months) to monitor progress and discuss any issues that have arisen.

CONCLUSION

This program can take participants from a traditional perspective of the role of the telephone interpreter as "still simply voice and ears for the deaf person" (Frishberg 1986, 170) to an acknowledgment that telephone interpreting is "one of the most challenging and frustrating tasks [interpreters] ever perform" because telephone calls are a hearing "cultural set based totally on sound" (Mindess 1991, 114).

Participants should begin to make explicit much of the innate knowledge they, as hearing people, have about the unspoken rules and protocols they observe in telephone conversations.

The program takes participants on a theoretical journey through widely used frameworks such as the conduit approach to more current thinking on interpreting (discourse interpreting), on translating (Venuti's issues of empowerment and cultural ownership [2000]), and in linguistics (critical discourse analysis).

One of the strengths of the program is that it does not seek to impose any particular routine for interpreted telephone exchanges; rather it seeks to encourage trainers and participants to consider the variety and complexity of types of telephone interactions and to develop an informed and flexible approach that allows the interpreter to adapt the practice of interpreting in situ, in consultation with the participants of the exchange.

We hope that trainers and their students will enjoy the program as much as we have and that they will enjoy the same kind of positive feedback from hearing and Deaf participants in interpreted telephone interaction. We welcome comments on the program, its application, and its results.

REFERENCES

Aijmer, K. 1996. *Conversational routines in English: Conventions and creativity.* New York: Addison West Longman.

Cheepen, C. 2000. Small talk in service dialogues: The conversational aspects of transactional telephone talk. In Coupland, J. (ed). *Small talk,* ed. J. Coupland, 288–311. Harlow, Essex, England: Pearson Education Limited.

Clark, H. H., and W. French. 1981. Telephone goodbyes. *Language in Society* 10:1–19.

Dickinson, J. 2002. Telephone interpreting: "Hello, is anybody there?" *Deaf Worlds* 18 (2):34–38.

Fairclough, N. 1995. *Critical discourse analysis: The critical study of language.* New York: Longman.

Frishberg, N. 1986. *Interpreting: An introduction.* Silver Spring, Md.: RID Publications.

Honey, P. 1986. *Telephone behaviour: The power and the perils* (booklet accompanying Video Arts video; see below). Watford, Hertfordshire, U.K.: B and H Printing Services.

Hopper, R. 1989. Speech in telephone openings: Emergent interaction v. routines. *Western Journal of Speech Communication* 53 :178–94.

Llewellyn-Jones, P. 1981. *BSL interpreting.* Paper presented to the third international sign language interpreters conference. Bristol University, London.

Luke, K. K., and Pavlidou, T.-S., eds. 2002. *Telephone calls.* Amsterdam: John Benjamins.

Metzger, M. 1999. *Sign language interpreting: Deconstructing the myth of neutrality.* Washington D.C.: Gallaudet University Press.

Mindess, A. 1991. *Reading between the signs: Intercultural communication for sign language interpreters.* Yarmouth, Maine: Intercultural Press.

Neuman-Solow, S. 1981. *Sign language interpreting: A basic resource book.* Silver Spring, Md.: NAD Publications.

Pollitt, K. 2000. Critical linguistic and cultural awareness: Essential tools in the interpreter's kit bag. In *Innovative practices for teaching sign language interpreters,* ed. C. Roy, 67–82. Washington, D.C.: Gallaudet University Press.

Timm, D. 2000. *Telephone interpreting.* American Sign Language Inter-
preting Resources:
http://asl_interpreting.tripod.com/situational_studies/dtl.htm.
Venuti, L. 1998. *The scandals of translation: Towards an ethic of difference.*
London: Routledge.
———. 2000. Translation, community, utopia. In *The translation studies
reader,* ed. L. Venuti, 468-89. London: Routledge.
Vermeer, H. J. 1989. Skopos and commission in translational action.
In *The Translation Studies Reader,* ed. L. Venuti, 221–33. London:
Routledge.
Video Arts. 1986. *Telephone behaviour: The power and the perils.* Video, di-
rected by Peter Robinson.
Wadensjö, C. 1999. Telephone interpreting and the synchronization of
talk in social interaction. *The Translator: Studies in Intercultural Com-
munication.* 5 (2):247–64.
Whalen, J., M. Whalen, and K. Henderson. 2002. Improvisational chore-
ography in telesales work. *British Journal of Sociology* 53:239-58.

INDEX

adequacy
    discourse mapping and, 53–55, 61, 64–68
American Sign Language (ASL)
    dynamic equivalence, 70, 72–73
    in-focus referents, 83–89
    referencing in, 79
    source attribution, 110–13
anthropology, 24
ASL. *See* American Sign Language
attention-getting strategies, 103–4, 117–18
audio material, 17–18
Australian Sign Language (Auslan), 123

background information, 107
blended space, 84–88
body shift, 110–11, 113
Boston University, 9
British Sign Language (BSL), 89

chaired multiparty meetings
    role of interpreters in, 157–63
    self-selection and source attribution,
        160–62
    teaching interpretational skills for, 163–68
    turn-taking in, 153–57
CIT. *See* Conference of Interpreter Trainers
clarification requests, 107, 117–18
classroom
    summonses and, 104
closings, 196, 198
cognates, 183
Cokely's model. *See* sociolinguistic model
communicative competence, 25
conduit interpretation, 189, 202
Conference of Interpreter Trainers (CIT),
    1–2, 3
confirmations, 196, 198

conscious omissions, 125
consecutive interpretation, 2, 14, 16
content
    discourse mapping and, 49, 64–68
context
    discourse analysis and, 24–25
    discourse mapping and, 49, 64–68
    pronouns and, 78
    referring expressions and, 91–92
control options, 30
controls, 29–30
conversational phone calls, 196
cooperative principle, 81–82
critical discourse analysis, 197–99
cross-talk, 193
curriculum revision, Northeastern
        University
    analysis of employment settings, 8–13
    details of, 13–20
    theoretical and philosophical influences,
        1–7

DawnSign Press, 116
D-C schema. *See* Demand-Control schema
Deaf community
    sign language interpreters and, 5–6
décalage, 202
Demand-Control (D-C) schema
    curricular collaboration and
        implementation, 30
    demand-control course, 33–34
    EIPI template, 28–29
    interpreter controls, 29–30
    observation enhancement program, 30–34
    observation-supervision teaching, 39–42
    simulated observation activities, 34–39
    value of, 42–44
dialogues, 6–7

211

digital video, 93
discourse
    impact of interpreters on, 100–01
discourse analysis, 24–25
discourse-centered curriculum, 14–20
discourse mapping
    adequacy and, 53–55, 61, 64–68
    assessing student translations, 60–73
    equivalency and, 53–55, 61–63, 68–73
    explanation of process, 50–52
    goals of, 51–52
    objections to, 54–55
    overview of, 49–50
    random concept maps, 57–59, 62–63
    sequential maps, 59–60
    student interpreters, 56–57
    student thoughts on, 73–76
    translation in, 55–56
dynamic equivalency, 68–73

Educational Interpreting course, 39–40
Effective Interpretation Series, 116
EIPI template
    description of, 28–29
    simulated observation activities, 34–39
employment
    settings and placements, 8–13
empowerment, 189, 193
English
    source attribution, 113–14
equivalence-based interpreting, 134
equivalency
    discourse mapping and, 53–55, 61–63,
        68–73
Ethical Fieldwork course, 18
ethnography
    anthropology and, 24
    applications, 27
    of communication, 25–26, 47–48
    discourse analysis, 24–25
    participant observation, 26–28
    primary objective, 26
"evolved" interpreters, 5–6
expert groups activity, 36
expository interactions, 11–12, 14
eye gaze, 89, 111, 113

false friends
    definitions of, 171–72, 180

effect on second-language learners,
    177–79
English-Swedish, 179–80
exercises for becoming aware of, 182–85
glosses and, 174
language proficiency and, 181
linguistic awareness and, 182–83, 185
non-Swedish mouth movements and,
    176–77
origins of, 179
problems for sign language learners,
    180–81
sign language interpreting and, 181–82
sign language teaching and, 173–74
simultaneous interpreting and, 182
Swedish mouth movements and, 174–75
false utopia concept, 201–02
faux amis. *See* false friends
first person pronouns, 107
    in interpreted telephone interactions,
        201–2
fixed referential framework, 89
foreignizing process, 202–03
fossilization, 90
Frog, Where Are You? (Mayer), 84–88, 93–97
Fund for the Improvement of Post-
    Secondary Education, 30

glosses, 57–58, 74
    non-Swedish mouth movements and,
        176–77
    Swedish false friends and, 174
    Swedish Sign Language and, 181
goal-to-detail and detail-to-goal teaching,
    62
greetings, 184
grounded blended space, 84–88

indexing, 111–13
in-focus referents, 83–89
information
    given and new, 80
inquiry interactions, 11–12, 14
interpreted interaction
    features of, 101–2
    introductions, 102–03
    overview of, 119
    pronominal reference, 107–8
    requests for clarification, 107

responses to questions, 105–6
source attribution, 108–18
summonses, 103–4
turn-taking and overlap, 104–5
interpreted telephone interactions. *See also*
    telephone interpreting
complexity of, 189–90
empowerment and, 189
first person pronoun in, 201–2
foreignizing process and, 202–3
interpreter as mediator, 203–7
interpreter as operator, 203, 207
issues surrounding, 188–90
metanotative qualities, 201
perspective of Deaf participants, 200–01
sound medium and, 187
unrealized utopia concept, 201–2
Interpreter Models Series, 4
interpreter preparation program (IPP)
observation enhancement program,
    30–34
observation-supervision teaching, 39–42
overview of, 30
simulated observation activities, 34–39
interpreter programs. *See also* individual
    programs
curriculum revision, 1–20
monologue interpreting, 3–5
temporal synchrony and, 2
interpreters
controls and, 29–30
discourse mapping and, 56–57
"evolved," 5–6
failure to recognize referents, 79
impact on discourse, 100–01
introductions, 102–3, 118–19
linguistic choices, 135
as mediator/operator, 203–7
questions and, 105–6, 117–18
relationship with Deaf community, 5–6
use of pronouns, 107–8
interpreting. *See also* interpreted interaction;
    simultaneous interpreting;
    telephone interpreting
conduit, 189, 202
consecutive, 2, 14, 16
dialogue, 6–7
monologue, 3–5
Interpreting in Insurance Settings, 116
Interpreting in Legal Settings, 116

Interpreting in Medical Settings, 116
Interpreting Inquiry Interactions course,
    16–17
Interpreting Persuasive Interactions course,
    18–19
introductions, 102–3, 118–19
teaching of, 117–18
IPP. *See* interpreter preparation program

large-group interactions, 9–10
linear maps. *See* sequential maps
linguistic awareness
false friends and, 170, 182–83, 185

Massachusetts Commission for the Deaf
    and Hard of Hearing, 8–9
Master Mentor Program, 56n
mediator
interpreter as, 203–7
medical education, 32
Medical Interpreting course, 39–42
medical interviews, 103–4, 114
metalinguistic awareness
defined, 123
omissions and, 123–24, 130–31, 135–36
miscue, 139n. 143
monitoring
classroom exercise, 145–49
decline in quality of, 143
defined, 141–42
monologue interpreting, 3–5
monologues
defined, 126
omission analysis and, 126
mouth movements. *See also* Swedish mouth
    movements
sign languages and, 172
multiparty meetings
role of interpreters in, 157–63
teaching interpretational skills for,
    163–68
turn-taking mechanisms, 152–57
written texts in, 162–63

naming
false friends and, 184
of sources, 112–13
narrative interaction, 11–12, 14

narrator framework, 89
National Multicultural Interpreting Project (NIMP), 26
NIMP. *See* National Multicultural Interpreting Project
Northeastern University
  curriculum revision, 1–20
Northern Essex Community College, 9

observation enhancement program, 30–34
observation skills, 30–34
observation-supervision teaching, 32–33, 39–42
observation techniques
  Demand-Control schema, 28–44
  discourse analysis, 24–25
  ethnography of communication, 25–26, 47–48
  introduction to, 22–23
  overview of, 24–28
omission potential, 123–24, 131–32
omissions
  analysis of, 124, 126–35
  identifying, 123
  interpreting, 124–26
  metalinguistic awareness and, 123–24, 130–31, 135–36
  statistical analysis, 135
  taxonomy, 125–26
one-to-many-many-to-one dilemma, 52–53
one-to-one interactions, 9–10
openings, 196, 198
operator
  interpreter as, 203, 207
overlap, 104–5, 141
  teaching of, 117–18

participant observation, 26–28
PBL. *See* problem-based learning
persuasive interactions, 11–12, 14
phatics, 193
picture analysis, 34–35
pictures
  discourse mapping and, 57–59, 74
positive self-talk, 30
practicum course
  in discourse-centered curriculum, 19–20
problem-based learning (PBL), 32

process management, 144
process monitoring, 142
pronominal reference, 107–8
  teaching of, 117–18
pronouns
  context and, 78
  in interpreted telephone interactions, 201–2
  interpreter use of, 107–8

qualitative research. *See* ethnography
questions
  to interpreters, 105–6, 117–18

random concept maps, 57–59, 62–63
real space, 83
real-time interpreting, 2
reference, 80–82. *See also* referring expressions
referents
  in-focus, 83–89
referring expressions
  in ASL, 79
  background information on reference, 80–82
  Frog, Where Are You? exercise, 93–97
  in-focus referents, 83–89
  level of interpreting skill and, 90
  observation and analysis of, 90–93
  second-language learners and, 78–79
  value of understanding, 98
Reforming Interpreter Education project, 30
Registry of Interpreters for the Deaf (RID), 2–4, 8
relevance theory, 81–82
Research Capstone course, 18
resource allocation, 144
RID. *See* Registry of Interpreters for the Deaf
roleplays
  in teaching source attribution, 117–18
  in telephone interpreter training, 204–5
role shifting, 83, 89

second-language learners
  false friends and, 177–79
  referring expressions and, 78–79

sequential maps
    in assessing content and context, 64–68
    assessing student translations and, 62–64
    created from random maps, 59, 63
shifted referential framework, 89
sign languages
    mouth movements and, 172
sign language teaching
    false friends and, 173–74
Sign Media, 4
Sign-to-Voice Interpretation course, 5
simulated observation activities, 34–39
simultaneous interpreting, 2
    in discourse-centered curriculum, 14, 16
    false friends and, 182
    problem of reference, 83–89
    source attribution, 109
skill development
    in discourse-centered curriculum, 17
skill-set sequences, 2–3, 5, 7
small-group interactions, 9–10, 108–9
sociolinguistic model
    classroom exercise, 143–49
    discussing with students, 140–41
    monitoring concept, 141–43
    outline of, 140
    value as a teaching model, 139–40
source attribution
    in ASL, 110–13
    in English, 113–14
    overview of, 108
    in simultaneous interpretation, 109
    in small-group interactions, 108–9
    teaching of, 114–18
SPEAKING acronym, 25–26, 47–48
story space, 83
summonses, 103–4
    teaching of, 117–18
swearwords, 178, 183
Swedish mouth movements
    false friends and, 174–75
    genuine, 176–77
    second-language learners and, 177–79
    Swedish Sign Language and, 172–75
Swedish Sign Language
    false friends and, 173–82
    glosses and, 174, 181
    non-Swedish mouth movements, 176–77
    problems for learners, 180–81
    second-language learners, 177–79

spoken Swedish and, 172
    Swedish mouth movements and, 172–76,
        179
synonyms, 182

telecommunications, 118
telephone calls, 195–99
telephone interpreter training
    becoming aware of Deaf participants,
        200–01
    critical discourse analysis, 197–99
    critical literature review, 191–93
    critiquing and deconstruction of
        interactions, 193–95
    discussing the future of, 207–8
    learning from telephone professionals,
        199–200
    listening to phone calls, 195–99
    overview of, 190–91
    roleplaying, 204–5
telephone interpreting. See also interpreted
        telephone interactions
    conduit approach, 189, 202
    décalage, 202
    issues surrounding, 188–90
    training material, 190–208
telephones
    services accessible through, 188
television show activity, 35–36
text analysis. See discourse mapping
textual foreignizing, 202–3
theoretical models. See also sociolinguistic
        model
    teaching of, 138–39, 149–50
"three-chair" exercise, 145–49
time lag, 202
transactional phone calls, 188, 196
translation
    in discourse-centered curriculum, 14, 16
    in discourse mapping, 55–56
    foreignizing process and, 202–3
    importance of, 50
    process of, 52–53
    testing the quality of, 54
translation decisions, 30
translation teaching. See discourse
        mapping
turn-taking, 104–5
    teaching of, 117–18

unconscious omissions, 126
United Kingdom, 189
University of Central Lancashire, 205
University of Rochester Medical Center, 30.
    See also UR-UT project
University of Tennessee, 30. *See also* UR-
    UT project
unrealized utopia concept, 201–2
UR-UT project
    observation enhancement program,
        30–34
    observation-supervision teaching, 39–42
    overview of, 30
    simulated observation activities, 34–39

video/video materials, 4
    in discourse-centered curriculum,
        17–18
    study of in-focus referents and, 92–93
    in study of omission analysis, 127, 128
    in teaching of source attribution,
        116–17
    in the "three-chair" exercise, 146
Voice-to-Sign Interpretation course, 5

war story analysis activity, 36–37